THE RHYTHMIC JOURNEY

UNLEASHING THE BEAT WITHIN

by Bart Robley

Foreword by
Dom Famularo

ISBN 978-1-57424-417-5

CENTERSTREAM®

P. O. Box 17878 - Anaheim Hills, CA 92817
email: centerstrm@aol.com • web: centerstream-usa.com

Music and rhythm find their way
into the secret places of the soul.

- Plato

Table of Contents

This book is dedicated to the memory of Drumming's Global Ambassador, Dom Famularo.

Foreword

Bart has put together a very different type of drum book. Very creative and needed - "The Rhythmic Journey: Unleashing the Beat Within." His vision is clear... to inspire future musicians with the wisdom of the importance of rhythmic understanding in our daily lives. There is a power in music... especially drumming! Bart guides you along the way of tapping into your potential!

He gives you an outline of what will assist you to better unleash your passion. Each topic is delivered in a helpful way to open opportunities for any musician. One of my favorites is Chapter 7, Discipline and Time Management through Drumming and Rhythm.

This is a lifelong journey and this book "The Rhythmic Journey: Unleashing the Beat Within" will be your guiderail to keep you on the best path. Finding your purpose is always a challenge, but Bart will hold your hand in each word. Step into Bart's world and enjoy your adventure in drumming!

Dom Famularo
Drumming's Global Ambassador

Watch Your Thoughts - They Become Words
Watch Your Words - They Become Actions
Watch Your Actions - They Become Habits
Watch Your Habits - They Become Character
Watch Your Character - For It Becomes Your Destiny.

- Dom Famularo

Chapter 1
Unleashing the Beat Within: The Power of Drums and Rhythm

In every corner of the world, the rhythmic pulse of drums has been an integral part of human culture and expression. From ancient tribal rituals to modern music genres, the power of drums and rhythm transcends time and connects us on a primal level. In this chapter, we explore the profound impact that drums and rhythm have on our lives, unleashing our innermost emotions, and fostering a sense of unity and belonging.

The power of drums and rhythm is a universal language that transcends cultural boundaries and connects people on a deep and primal level. Throughout history, drums have been used in various cultures around the world for communication, ceremony, and celebration. The rhythmic patterns created by drums have the ability to evoke strong emotions, energize individuals, and unite communities. Whether it's the pulsating beats of a traditional African djembe, the thunderous sounds of Japanese taiko drums, or the intricate rhythms of Latin American congas, drums have the power to captivate and transport listeners to a different state of being.

Rhythm, as a fundamental element of music, has a profound impact on human beings. It has been scientifically proven that rhythm has the ability to synchronize brainwaves, heart rate, and even breathing patterns. The repetitive and structured nature of rhythm creates a sense of order and stability, allowing individuals to connect with their bodies and surroundings. It has therapeutic effects, reducing stress and anxiety, and promoting relaxation and focus. The power of rhythm is evident in its ability to inspire movement, prompting people to dance, sway, or tap their feet involuntarily.

Drums, as the heartbeat of music, hold a special place in many cultures. They are often associated with spiritual rituals and ceremonies, where their powerful vibrations are believed to communicate with the divine. The deep, resonating tones of drums can awaken dormant energies and stir the soul. Whether it's the war drums of ancient warriors or the sacred rhythms of shamanic rituals, drums have the ability to transcend language and convey emotions and intentions in a way that words cannot. They awaken a primal instinct within us, connecting us to our ancestors and reminding us of our shared humanity.

The power of drums and rhythm lies in their ability to transcend cultural boundaries, synchronize our bodies and minds, and evoke deep emotions. They have been an integral part of human expression and communication throughout history, from ancient rituals to modern music genres. The beat of a drum can unite communities, bring joy and celebration, and create a sense of harmony and connection. So, whether you find yourself tapping your foot to a catchy rhythm or being moved by the thunderous sound of drums, embrace the power that these instruments hold and let them take you on a transformative journey.

The Universal Language of Rhythm

Rhythm is a universal language that surpasses linguistic barriers, cultural differences, and geographical distances. It speaks directly to the core of our being, bypassing the complexities of spoken communication. Drums, with their primal beats and pulsating rhythms, serve as the heartbeat of this universal language. They possess the power to evoke emotions, ignite passion, and create a bridge between individuals and communities.

Rhythm is often referred to as the universal language of music because it has the remarkable ability to transcend cultural and linguistic barriers. Regardless of where one comes from or what language they speak, the power of rhythm can be understood and appreciated by people from all walks of life. It is a primal force that resonates within us, connecting us on a fundamental level. The rhythmic patterns and structures found in music can convey emotions, tell stories, and convey messages without the need for words. This universality of rhythm allows for cross-cultural collaborations, where musicians from different backgrounds can come together and create something harmonious and cohesive, despite their differences.

Furthermore, rhythm extends beyond music and permeates various aspects of our daily lives. From the beating of our hearts to the cycles of nature, rhythm is an inherent part of the world around us. We instinctively respond to rhythm, whether it's through our movement, our breathing, or our sense of timing. It influences the way we speak, walk, and interact with others. This innate connection to rhythm allows us to communicate and connect with one another in a profound way, even when we don't share a common language. It is a language of the body and the soul, capable of transcending barriers and fostering unity among people of diverse backgrounds.

The Healing Power of Drumming

Drumming has long been recognized as a powerful therapeutic tool, capable of promoting healing and well-being. When we engage in drumming, our bodies synchronize with the rhythm, inducing a state of relaxation and reducing stress levels. The act of drumming releases endorphins, neurotransmitters that enhance our mood and alleviate pain. The repetitive nature of drumming also aids in achieving a meditative state, promoting mindfulness and inner peace.

Furthermore, drumming has been found to have profound effects on mental health. It offers an outlet for emotional expression, allowing individuals to release pent-up feelings and find solace in the cathartic nature of the beats. Drum circles, where people come together to create rhythmic music, foster a sense of belonging and connection, reducing feelings of isolation and loneliness.

The healing power of drumming and rhythm has been recognized and utilized for centuries in various cultures around the world. Engaging in drumming and rhythmic activities has been found to have significant mental and physical benefits. From a mental health perspective, drumming can be a powerful form of self-expression and release. The act of drumming allows individuals to channel their emotions and release stress and tension. It provides an outlet for creativity and promotes a sense of empowerment and control. Drumming in a group setting also fosters a sense of community and connection, reducing feelings of loneliness and isolation.

On a physical level, drumming and rhythm have been shown to have therapeutic effects. The repetitive movements involved in drumming can induce a state of relaxation, reducing blood pressure and heart rate. It can also help improve coordination, motor skills, and cognitive function. Drumming is a full-body experience that engages the muscles, improves dexterity, and stimulates the brain. It has been used as a therapeutic tool in various settings, such as rehabilitation centers and support groups, to aid in physical rehabilitation, pain management, and overall well-being.

Moreover, drumming and rhythm have the ability to positively impact the brain and promote mental well-being. Studies have shown that drumming activates both hemispheres of the brain, fostering neural connections and enhancing cognitive function. It can improve focus, concentration, and memory. Drumming also stimulates the production of endorphins and serotonin, neurotransmitters associated with positive emotions and feelings of happiness. The rhythmic nature of drumming can help individuals enter a meditative state, reducing anxiety and promoting mindfulness. It provides an avenue for self-care and self-expression, allowing individuals to reconnect with themselves and find inner peace.

Drumming and rhythm have profound healing effects on both the mind and body. They offer a holistic approach to well-being, addressing mental, emotional, and physical aspects of health. Whether it's through stress relief, fostering community, enhancing physical coordination, or promoting mental clarity, the healing power of drumming and rhythm is a testament to the innate connection between music and our overall well-being. So, the next time you find yourself drawn to the beat of a drum, embrace its therapeutic potential and let the rhythm guide you on a path of healing and self-discovery.

The Power of Collective Rhythm

When we gather as a collective to drum, we tap into a primal instinct that unites us all. The power of collective rhythm is transformative, as it dissolves barriers and creates a sense of unity among diverse groups of people. In drum circles, individual egos fade away as participants merge their beats into a cohesive rhythm. The experience transcends the boundaries of age, race, and social status, highlighting our shared humanity.

The collective rhythm also has the power to create a sense of empowerment and drive social change. Throughout history, drums have been used as a tool for communication during protests and revolutions, carrying the pulse of a united voice demanding justice and freedom. The beat of the drums instills courage and determination, inspiring individuals to stand up for what they believe in.

The power of collective rhythm lies in its ability to bring people together and create a sense of unity and cohesion. When individuals join together in creating a shared rhythm, whether through drumming circles, music ensembles, or even synchronized clapping and chanting, a powerful synergy emerges. The combined energy and synchronized

movements create a palpable sense of connection and belonging. It transcends individual differences and fosters a collective experience that is greater than the sum of its parts. The power of collective rhythm can be felt in various contexts, from cultural celebrations and religious ceremonies to social movements and protests, where the rhythmic pulse acts as a unifying force, amplifying the collective voice.

Collective rhythm has the ability to transcend language and cultural barriers, allowing for communication and understanding beyond words. It provides a common language that everyone can participate in, regardless of their background or experiences. Through the shared experience of rhythm, barriers are broken down, and individuals are able to connect and empathize with one another. The power of collective rhythm lies in its ability to create a safe and inclusive space where everyone's voice is heard and valued. It fosters a sense of belonging and empowers individuals to express themselves freely and authentically.

Moreover, collective rhythm has the potential to create a transformative and uplifting experience. When individuals synchronize their movements and intentions, a powerful energy is generated. The combined rhythm has the capacity to create a positive and uplifting atmosphere, evoking emotions of joy, unity, and empowerment. It can inspire individuals to move and dance, to let go of inhibitions and be fully present in the moment. The power of collective rhythm can generate a sense of shared purpose and ignite a collective spirit that can be harnessed for positive change and transformation, both individually and within communities.

The power of collective rhythm is a testament to the human capacity for connection, unity, and transformation. It transcends language and cultural boundaries, fostering communication and understanding. It has the ability to create a sense of belonging and empower individuals to express themselves authentically. The collective energy generated through rhythm can be transformative, uplifting, and inspiring. So, whether it's through drumming circles, musical collaborations, or synchronized movements, let us embrace the power of collective rhythm and allow it to unite us and amplify our voices for positive change.

Expressing Emotions Through Drumming

Drumming provides an avenue for emotional expression that surpasses the limitations of words. It allows us to give voice to our innermost emotions, whether it be joy, sorrow, anger, or love. The rhythmic patterns we create on the drums serve as a canvas upon which we can paint our

feelings, translating the intangible into something tangible and palpable.

Beyond personal expression, drumming also enables us to communicate and connect with others on an emotional level. In a drum circle or a band, each player contributes their unique rhythms, harmonizing with others to create a vibrant tapestry of sound. Through this shared musical dialogue, we develop empathy, understanding, and a deeper appreciation for the diversity of human experiences.

Drums and rhythm possess an innate power to awaken our souls and unleash the beat within us. They transcend boundaries, heal wounds, foster unity, and provide a medium for emotional expression. Whether we drum alone or in a collective, the transformative potential of rhythm is undeniable. So, let us embrace the power of drums, tap into our primal instincts, and allow the beat to resonate within us, connecting us to ourselves, each other, and the world around us.

Expressing emotions through drumming and rhythm is a powerful and cathartic experience. The rhythmic patterns and beats created by drumming have the ability to evoke and amplify a wide range of emotions. Whether it's the pounding rhythms that convey anger and frustration or the gentle and soothing rhythms that express tranquility and peace, drumming provides a means to channel and release emotions that may be difficult to put into words. The act of drumming allows individuals to connect with their innermost feelings and express them in a raw and authentic way.

Drumming and rhythm can serve as a non-verbal language for emotional expression. Sometimes, emotions can be overwhelming or hard to articulate verbally, but through the language of rhythm, individuals can communicate and convey their emotions without the need for words. The power of drumming lies in its ability to bypass the rational mind and tap into the primal and intuitive aspects of our being. It allows individuals to create a sonic landscape that mirrors their emotional state, providing a safe and supportive outlet for emotional release and exploration.

Engaging in drumming and rhythm can also facilitate emotional healing and processing. By allowing emotions to flow freely through the act of drumming, individuals can release pent-up feelings and experience a sense of catharsis. Drumming can help individuals process and transform negative emotions into positive ones. It provides a healthy and constructive means of emotional release, promoting emotional well-being and inner balance.

Furthermore, drumming in a group setting can create a space for collective emotional expression and connection. When individuals come together to drum, they form a collective energy that amplifies and resonates with each other's emotions. The shared experience of drumming can foster a sense of empathy and understanding among participants. It creates a supportive and non-judgmental environment where individuals can express their emotions and feel validated and heard by others. Drum circles and group drumming sessions offer a unique opportunity for emotional connection and communal healing.

Drumming and rhythm provide a powerful medium for expressing and exploring emotions. They offer a non-verbal language that can communicate and amplify a wide range of feelings. Through drumming, individuals can connect with their inner emotions, release pent-up feelings, and experience catharsis. Drumming in a group setting also fosters collective emotional expression and creates a sense of community. So, whether you're drumming alone or participating in a group drumming session, embrace the power of rhythm to express and navigate the rich tapestry of human emotions.

The power of rhythm is a profound force that transcends boundaries, connects people, and provides a gateway to self-expression and emotional release. Whether through the pounding beats of a drum or the intricate patterns of a musical ensemble, rhythm has the ability to move us, both physically and emotionally. It has therapeutic effects, promoting relaxation, healing, and a sense of unity. The universal language of rhythm brings people together, creating a collective experience that can be transformative and uplifting.

In the next chapter, we will explore the fascinating realm of developing coordination and motor skills through drumming and rhythm. Engaging in rhythmic activities requires a high degree of coordination between the hands, feet, and body. Drumming provides an excellent platform to enhance motor skills, as it requires precise timing, limb independence, and fine motor control. We will delve into various techniques, exercises, and strategies that can be employed to develop coordination and motor skills through drumming. Whether you are a beginner or an experienced drummer, this chapter will provide valuable insights and practical tips to take your rhythmic abilities to new heights. Get ready to embark on a rhythmic journey that will not only improve your drumming skills but also enhance your overall coordination and motor abilities.

Chapter 2
Developing Coordination and Motor Skills Through Drumming and Rhythm

Drumming and rhythm have long been recognized as powerful tools for developing coordination and motor skills. From ancient tribal cultures to modern music therapy practices, the act of drumming engages the mind, body, and spirit in a unique and holistic way. In this chapter, we will explore the benefits of drumming for coordination and motor skill development, discuss the underlying mechanisms at work, and provide practical strategies for incorporating drumming and rhythm into your daily routine.

The Benefits of Drumming For Coordination and Motor Skills

Drumming requires the synchronization of multiple limbs and fine motor control, making it an excellent activity for enhancing coordination and motor skills. Drumming is not only a thrilling and engaging musical activity, but it also offers a wide range of benefits for coordination and motor skills development. Whether you're a professional drummer or someone who enjoys drumming as a hobby, the rhythmic patterns and physical movements involved in playing drums can have a profound impact on your coordination, dexterity, and overall motor skills. From improving hand-eye coordination to enhancing fine motor control, drumming provides a unique avenue for individuals of all ages to enhance their physical abilities while immersing themselves in the world of music.

One of the key advantages of drumming is its ability to enhance coordination skills. When playing the drums, individuals must synchronize their hands, feet, and sometimes even other body parts to produce rhythmic patterns and beats. This requires precise timing, concentration, and the ability to coordinate movements between different limbs. As drummers develop their skills, they gradually learn to perform complex rhythmic patterns, cross-limb coordination exercises, and polyrhythms, which significantly improve their overall coordination abilities. These skills not only benefit drummers in their musical endeavors but also have practical applications in various daily activities that involve coordination, such as sports, dance, and even everyday tasks like typing or cooking.

Here are some key benefits of drumming:

1. MOTOR COORDINATION: Drumming involves the coordinated movement of hands, feet, and sometimes even the entire body. By practicing drumming exercises, individuals can improve their ability to perform complex movements with precision and timing.

Drumming is a powerful tool for developing motor coordination, particularly when it comes to rhythm. When playing the drums, individuals must learn to synchronize their movements with the beat and maintain a steady rhythm. This requires precise timing, control, and the ability to coordinate multiple limbs simultaneously. Drummers develop a keen sense of rhythm through constant practice and repetition, which strengthens the neural connections between their brains and muscles. As a result, their motor coordination skills are honed, and they become adept at executing intricate patterns and maintaining consistent tempo.

Moreover, drumming engages both fine and gross motor skills, offering a comprehensive workout for the entire body. Drummers use their hands and fingers to strike different parts of the drum kit, producing distinct sounds and rhythms. This intricate fingerwork improves fine motor skills, dexterity, and hand-eye coordination. Additionally, footwork is crucial for controlling bass drum pedals and hi-hat cymbals, which enhances gross motor skills and coordination between the hands and feet. The combination of these movements challenges the brain to coordinate various muscle groups simultaneously, leading to improved overall motor coordination abilities.

The benefits of drumming extend beyond the technical aspects of motor coordination. Drumming also has a positive impact on cognitive functions such as focus, attention, and memory, which are closely tied to motor coordination. When playing the drums, individuals must concentrate on maintaining the rhythm, anticipating upcoming beats, and coordinating their movements accordingly. This requires mental focus and attention to detail. The repetitive nature of drumming patterns also enhances memory and pattern recognition skills. As drummers internalize different rhythms and techniques, they develop a mental database of patterns, which allows them to execute complex rhythms

Bart Robley

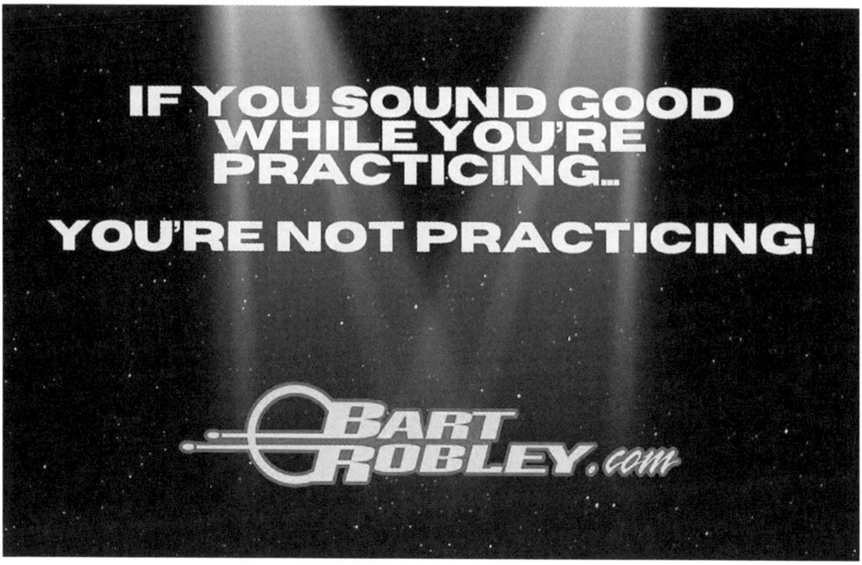

effortlessly. By engaging both the mind and body, drumming fosters a holistic approach to motor coordination development.

2. FINE MOTOR SKILLS: The manipulation of drumsticks or hand drumming techniques requires refined finger and hand movements. Regular drumming practice can enhance dexterity, finger independence, and control over small muscles, which can have positive effects on activities requiring fine motor skills. Drumming and rhythm play a significant role in the development of fine motor skills. When playing the drums, drummers engage in precise and controlled movements of their hands, fingers, and wrists to strike different parts of the drum kit. This intricate fingerwork improves fine motor skills, dexterity, and hand-eye coordination. Drummers must develop the ability to strike the drumheads with varying degrees of force and precision, producing different sounds and tones. This level of control requires the refinement of fine motor skills, allowing drummers to execute complex patterns and express themselves artistically through their drumming.

Furthermore, drumming offers a unique opportunity to enhance finger independence and coordination. Drummers often practice rudiments and exercises that involve specific finger movements, such as rolls, flams, and paradiddles. These exercises require precise coordination between individual fingers and promote the development of fine motor skills. Over time, drummers develop the ability to execute these movements effortlessly and fluidly, resulting in improved finger dexterity and control. The combination of rhythm and fine motor skill development in drumming provides a comprehensive workout for the hands and fingers, fostering the refinement of motor skills essential for various activities beyond drumming, such as writing, playing instruments, and engaging in delicate tasks.

3. BILATERAL INTEGRATION: Drumming often involves playing different patterns with each hand or foot simultaneously. This promotes bilateral integration, allowing the brain to efficiently communicate and coordinate movements between both sides of the body. Drumming, with its rhythmic patterns and complex movements, offers significant benefits for bilateral integration, which refers to the coordination and communication between the left and right sides of the body. When playing the drums, drummers utilize both hands and feet simultaneously, creating a symphony of coordinated movements. This engagement of both sides of the body strengthens the neural connections between the brain hemispheres, promoting effective communication and synchronization between them. As a result, drumming enhances bilateral integration skills, which have a wide range of applications in everyday activities.

One of the key benefits of drumming for bilateral integration is improved hand-eye coordination. Drummers must watch their drumsticks while striking different drums and cymbals, requiring precise timing and accuracy. This visual input is processed by the brain, which sends signals to the hands and fingers to execute the corresponding movements. By consistently practicing drumming and rhythm, individuals develop a heightened sense of hand-eye coordination, as the brain becomes adept at processing visual information and translating it into coordinated motor responses. This enhanced coordination extends beyond drumming and can positively impact various tasks that require visual-motor integration, such as playing sports, driving, or even handwriting.

Drumming also strengthens the connection between the hands and feet, facilitating better coordination and synchronization. Drummers often employ bass drum pedals and hi-hat cymbals, which involve simultaneous footwork with hand movements. Coordinating the actions of both hands and feet requires the brain to process and coordinate signals effectively, fostering bilateral integration. As drummers progress, they develop the ability to execute intricate patterns and syncopated rhythms, showcasing their enhanced bilateral coordination. This skill translates to other activities that involve coordinating movements between the hands and feet, such as dancing, playing sports, or even walking while carrying objects.

Moreover, drumming and rhythm promote overall brain integration, as various brain regions are engaged in the complex task of coordinating movements and processing rhythmic patterns. Research has shown that rhythmic activities, like drumming, stimulate the brain's motor and auditory areas, improving neural connectivity and fostering brain integration. This enhanced connectivity has a positive impact on cognitive functions such as attention, memory, and problem-solving. By engaging the brain in a rhythmic and coordinated manner, drumming supports the development of bilateral integration at a neurological level, leading to improved overall brain function and cognitive abilities.

Drumming and rhythm provide numerous benefits for bilateral integration. By engaging both sides of the body and fostering coordination between the hands, feet, and visual input, drummers enhance hand-eye coordination, strengthen the connection between hands and feet, and promote overall brain integration. These skills extend beyond the realm of drumming, benefiting individuals in various aspects of their lives that require coordinated movements and effective communication between different body parts. Whether pursuing drumming as a hobby or profession, the rewards of improved bilateral integration through drumming are far-reaching and impactful.

4. RHYTHM PERCEPTION: Drumming is deeply connected to rhythm, and the ability to perceive and reproduce rhythmic patterns is crucial for coordination. Through drumming, individuals develop a heightened sense of timing, beat awareness, and rhythmic accuracy. Drumming and rhythm perception go hand in hand, and both offer significant benefits for individuals. Engaging in drumming activities helps develop a heightened sense of rhythm perception, which refers to the ability to perceive and interpret rhythmic patterns accurately. Drummers train their ears to identify and reproduce various rhythms, beats, and accents, which in turn improves their overall sense of rhythm perception. This skill extends beyond drumming and has practical applications in music, dance, and everyday activities where a strong sense of timing and rhythm is required.

One of the key advantages of drumming for rhythm perception is the development of an internalized sense of timing. As drummers practice and play along with metronomes or other musicians, they learn to

internalize the steady pulse and synchronize their playing accordingly. This process enhances their ability to perceive and anticipate rhythmic patterns, as they become attuned to the underlying pulse and subdivisions of beats. Drummers develop a keen sense of timing, allowing them to maintain a steady tempo and accurately interpret rhythmic cues in various musical contexts.

Drumming also improves rhythm perception by honing the ability to discern and reproduce complex rhythmic patterns. Drummers often practice exercises and techniques that involve intricate rhythms and polyrhythms, requiring them to perceive and reproduce complex patterns simultaneously. This process challenges the brain to analyze and interpret multiple rhythmic layers, strengthening the neural pathways associated with rhythm perception. As drummers progress, they become more adept at perceiving subtle rhythmic nuances and accents, enhancing their musicality and ability to express themselves through rhythm.

Furthermore, drumming enhances the brain's ability to synchronize with external rhythmic stimuli. Studies have shown that drumming promotes neural entrainment, a process in which the brain aligns its neural oscillations with external rhythms. This synchronization of brain activity with rhythmic stimuli enhances rhythm perception and can have positive effects on cognitive functions such as attention, memory, and auditory processing. Drummers often experience a state of "flow" while playing, where they are fully immersed in the rhythm and feel a deep connection with the music. This heightened state of engagement fosters a more profound and intuitive understanding of rhythm, further enhancing rhythm perception skills.

Drumming and rhythm perception are closely intertwined, with drumming serving as a powerful tool for developing a heightened sense of rhythm perception. By practicing and internalizing timing, discerning complex rhythmic patterns, and promoting neural entrainment, drummers enhance their ability to perceive and interpret rhythm accurately. These benefits extend beyond drumming and can positively impact various areas of life that involve rhythmic activities, such as music, dance, and everyday tasks that require a strong sense of timing and coordination.

Mechanisms at Work

When it comes to learning rhythm and drumming, the brain is a fascinating powerhouse of interconnected mechanisms that work together to process, analyze, and reproduce rhythmic patterns. The intricate process of learning rhythm and drumming involves various regions of the brain, including the auditory cortex, motor cortex, and cerebellum, among others. As individuals engage in the rhythmic world of drumming, neural pathways are formed, strengthened, and refined, leading to improved timing, coordination, and musicality. Understanding the brain's mechanisms at work during rhythm and drumming learning provides insight into the remarkable cognitive processes involved in mastering this rhythmic art form. Drumming engages various brain regions and neural pathways involved in motor coordination and skill development. Here are some of the underlying mechanisms:

1. **NEUROPLASTICITY:** Drumming stimulates neuroplasticity, which is brain's remarkable ability to change and adapt in response to experiences, learning, and environmental influences. the brain's ability to reorganize and form new connections. Regular practice strengthens existing neural pathways and creates new ones, improving coordination and motor skills. It involves the formation of new neural connections, the strengthening of existing connections, and even the reorganization of brain regions. Drumming and rhythm have been shown to have a profound

impact on neuroplasticity by stimulating and enhancing brain plasticity. When individuals engage in drumming activities, they challenge their brains to process complex rhythmic patterns, coordinate movements, and integrate auditory and motor information. These repeated and focused rhythmic experiences create a fertile ground for neuroplasticity to occur.

Drumming and rhythm engage multiple brain regions simultaneously, leading to increased synaptic connections and neural network growth. The auditory cortex, responsible for processing sound, becomes finely tuned to distinguish and interpret rhythmic patterns and musical nuances. Meanwhile, the motor cortex, responsible for controlling movement, undergoes changes as drummers develop the coordination and motor skills necessary to play the drums. These regions communicate and synchronize their activities, fostering the rewiring and strengthening of neural pathways.

Moreover, drumming and rhythm stimulate the release of neurochemicals and growth factors that facilitate neuroplasticity. The engagement with rhythm and music triggers the release of dopamine, a neurotransmitter associated with pleasure, reward, and motivation. This dopamine release reinforces the brain's connection between the enjoyment of drumming and the desire to continue practicing, thus promoting further neuroplastic changes. Additionally, drumming stimulates the production of brain-derived neurotrophic factor (BDNF), a protein crucial for the growth, survival, and function of neurons. Increased levels of BDNF facilitate the growth of new connections between brain cells and support the adaptability of the brain, ultimately enhancing neuroplasticity.

Drumming and rhythm play a significant role in promoting neuroplasticity by engaging multiple brain regions, fostering the formation of new neural connections, and stimulating the release of neurochemicals that support brain adaptability. By actively participating in rhythmic experiences, individuals harness the brain's remarkable capacity for change and growth. This not only leads to improved musical skills but also benefits cognitive functions, emotional well-being, and overall brain health.

2. SYNCHRONIZATION: Drumming requires precise synchronization of motor actions with auditory stimuli. This synchronization strengthens the connections between auditory and motor regions of the brain, facilitating better coordination. Drumming and rhythm have a profound impact on synchronization in the human brain. When a person engages in drumming or listens to rhythmic music, the brain's neural networks responsible for processing auditory and motor information become highly active. This activation stimulates various regions of the brain, including the auditory cortex, motor cortex, and basal ganglia, which are involved in rhythm perception and motor coordination. As a result, drumming and rhythm help synchronize different parts of the brain, leading to enhanced cognitive function and improved neural connectivity.

One key mechanism through which drumming and rhythm facilitate synchronization in the human brain is through entrainment. Entrainment refers to the process by which external rhythms influence and synchronize internal bodily rhythms. When drumming or rhythmic patterns are perceived by the brain, the auditory cortex detects the temporal structure and sends signals to the motor cortex, which coordinates movement accordingly. This synchronization between perception and action strengthens the neural connections between auditory and motor regions, promoting efficient communication and coordination within the brain. Moreover, the repetitive nature of drumming and rhythm stimulates the release of neurotransmitters like dopamine, which further enhances neural plasticity and facilitates synchronization in the brain. As a result, drumming and rhythm have the power to foster synchronization, improve motor skills, enhance cognitive abilities, and promote overall well-being.

3. **CROSS-HEMISPHERIC COMMUNICATION:** Drumming involves the simultaneous use of both hemispheres of the brain. This enhances communication and coordination between the left and right hemispheres, promoting overall motor skill development. Drumming and rhythm play a significant role in promoting cross-hemispheric communication in the human brain. When a person engages in drumming or listens to rhythmic music, both hemispheres of the brain are activated and communicate with each other. The rhythmic patterns and beats stimulate the auditory cortex in the left hemisphere, which processes the temporal aspects of sound. Simultaneously, the motor cortex in the right hemisphere is engaged as it coordinates the movement of drumming. This cross-hemispheric interaction strengthens the connections between the two hemispheres, facilitating communication and integration of information.

The corpus callosum, a dense bundle of nerve fibers connecting the left and right hemispheres, plays a crucial role in cross-hemispheric communication. Drumming and rhythm have been found to enhance the functioning and integrity of the corpus callosum. As the brain processes and responds to rhythmic stimuli, the information is shared across both hemispheres through this neural bridge. The synchronization of neural activity between the hemispheres fosters a more balanced and integrated brain function, leading to improved cognitive abilities, creativity, and problem-solving skills.

Moreover, drumming and rhythm engage multiple sensory and motor systems in the brain. When a person plays drums or engages in rhythmic activities, they integrate visual, auditory, and motor information. This multimodal engagement stimulates various brain regions, including the occipital, temporal, and parietal lobes, resulting in enhanced cross-hemispheric communication. By involving multiple brain systems simultaneously, drumming and rhythm promote holistic brain functioning, allowing for the efficient exchange of information and the integration of different cognitive processes.

Practical Strategies for Developing Coordination and Motor Skills through Drumming

Now that we understand the benefits and mechanisms behind drumming's impact on coordination and motor skills, let's explore some practical strategies to incorporate drumming into your routine:

1. START WITH BASIC RHYTHMS: Begin by practicing simple drumming patterns, focusing on maintaining a steady beat and coordinating your hands and feet. A basic rhythm or drum beat refers to the fundamental rhythmic pattern that forms the foundation of a musical composition. It serves as a consistent and repetitive pulse that provides a rhythmic framework for other instruments and elements to build upon. A basic rhythm typically consists of a sequence of evenly spaced beats, often played on a drum or percussion instrument. It establishes the tempo and meter of the music, creating a sense of groove and driving the overall rhythmic feel. The simplicity of a basic rhythm allows for easy comprehension and synchronization, making it accessible for musicians and listeners alike. While basic rhythms may vary across musical genres and cultures, they are universally recognized as essential building blocks that shape the structure and energy of a musical piece. As you progress, gradually introduce more complex rhythms and techniques.

MISTER RUDIMENTS
Ralph G. Eames, Jr.
Wakefield, Mass.
THE MAINE CHAMPION
Emile F. Cote
Old Orchard Beach, Maine
Other D
SCHOOL OF HARD ROCKS
MAKERS
1883

2. LIMB INDEPENDENCE EXERCISES: Engage in exercises that challenge each limb independently. For example, practice playing different rhythms with your left and right hands, or alternate between different foot patterns on the bass drum. Developing limb independence is a crucial skill for drummers and rhythm enthusiasts, as it allows them to play different rhythms or patterns with each limb simultaneously. Here are some effective ways to develop limb independence and improve coordination:

A. START WITH SIMPLE EXERCISES: Begin by practicing basic coordination exercises that involve playing different rhythms with each limb. For example, you can start with a simple exercise of playing a steady quarter-note pulse on the bass drum while simultaneously playing a snare drum pattern on the backbeat. Gradually increase the complexity of the exercises as you become more comfortable.

B. BREAK IT DOWN: When facing complex patterns, break them down into smaller parts and practice each limb independently. Start by mastering the pattern with one limb, and then gradually add in the other limbs. This approach allows you to focus on each limb's movement and timing, gradually building the muscle memory required for limb independence.

C. USE RHYTHMIC SUBDIVISIONS: Practice exercises that involve playing different subdivisions of the beat with each limb. For instance, you can play eighth notes on the hi-hat with one hand while playing quarter-note triplets on the bass drum with the other foot. This helps develop limb independence and rhythmic precision.

D. PLAY ALONG WITH MUSIC: Choose songs or drum tracks that have challenging rhythmic patterns and play along with them. This helps you apply your limb independence skills in a musical context and improves your ability to synchronize with other instruments.

Remember to start slow and gradually increase the speed as you become more comfortable. Consistent practice and patience are key to developing limb independence. By incorporating these exercises into your drumming routine, you will enhance your coordination, dexterity, and overall rhythmic abilities.

3. DRUMMING GAMES: Make drumming a fun and interactive experience by incorporating games. Play "call and response" exercises, where one person plays a rhythm, and others try to mimic it. This game enhances listening skills and promotes coordination.

Drumming games provide an interactive and engaging way to develop rhythm and musicality. These games often involve rhythmic patterns, coordination challenges, and a sense of playfulness. They can be played individually or in groups, fostering creativity, communication, and a deeper understanding of rhythm. Drumming games not only make the learning process enjoyable but also serve as effective tools for honing rhythmic skills and promoting musical expression.

"Call and response" is a rhythmic technique commonly used in drumming and various musical traditions worldwide. It involves a back-and-forth musical conversation between two or more players. In this rhythmic dialogue, one person (the "caller") initiates a rhythmic phrase or pattern, and the other person(s) (the "responders") immediately mimic or respond with a complementary phrase. This rhythmic call and response interaction creates a dynamic and interactive musical exchange, allowing musicians to communicate and improvise together.

Rhythmically, "call and response" relies on the synchronization and coordination of the participants. The caller establishes a rhythmic motif or phrase, emphasizing specific accents or patterns. The responders then listen attentively and reproduce the same rhythm or respond with a complementary phrase that complements or builds upon the initial call. This rhythmic interplay showcases the importance of active listening, timing, and precision in drumming and musical communication. "Call and response" not only enhances rhythmic skills but also fosters collaboration, improvisation, and a deeper sense of musical connection between participants.

4. GROUP DRUMMING SESSIONS: Join a drumming circle or take part in group drumming sessions. These activities provide opportunities for social interaction, cooperation, and synchronization with others, further enhancing coordination and motor skills. Group drumming sessions offer a unique and powerful platform for building drumming skills, rhythm, and social interaction. When individuals come together to play drums as a group, they have the opportunity to learn from one another, synchronize their rhythms, and create a cohesive musical experience. Group drumming allows participants to develop their drumming techniques, such as timing, dynamics, and coordination, by observing and emulating the skills of others. This collective learning environment fosters a supportive atmosphere where drummers can share their knowledge, experiment with different rhythms, and receive immediate feedback, all of which contribute to their growth as drummers.

In addition to building drumming skills, group drumming sessions also promote social interaction and a sense of community. Drumming together creates a shared experience that transcends cultural, linguistic, and social barriers. The collaborative nature of group drumming encourages participants to actively listen, communicate non-verbally through rhythm, and respond to the musical cues of others. This cooperative engagement cultivates a sense of unity, cooperation, and teamwork among the participants. Moreover, group drumming sessions often involve elements of improvisation, where individuals have the opportunity to express themselves creatively within the group context. This fosters self-expression, boosts confidence, and nurtures a sense of belonging, as individuals contribute to the collective rhythm and musical energy of the group. Overall, group drumming sessions not only enhance drumming skills and rhythm but also create a supportive and inclusive social space that promotes connection, communication, and personal growth.

5. MUSIC-BASED WORKOUTS: Incorporate drumming into your exercise routine. Participate in drumming fitness classes or use drumming as a rhythmic backdrop to your workout. The combination of movement and rhythm enhances overall coordination and motor skill development. Music-based workouts offer a multifaceted approach to improving physical fitness while simultaneously benefiting the human brain. Engaging in exercise routines accompanied by music has been shown to enhance cognitive function, memory, and attention span. The rhythmic nature of music-based workouts stimulates the brain's motor and auditory systems, promoting synchronization and coordination. Furthermore, the release of endorphins during physical activity, combined with the emotional and motivational aspects of music, can elevate mood, reduce stress, and increase overall well-being. These positive effects on the brain can enhance cognitive performance, creativity, and even support neuroplasticity.

Listening to music is an integral part of developing drumming skills. By actively listening to various genres and styles of music, drummers can absorb different rhythmic patterns, phrasing techniques, and musical

nuances. Music provides a rich and diverse repertoire of rhythms, tempos, and musical structures that drummers can draw inspiration from and incorporate into their playing. Additionally, actively listening to music helps drummers develop a keen sense of timing, dynamics, and musicality, enabling them to play with greater precision and sensitivity. Regular exposure to different genres of music expands their rhythmic vocabulary and exposes them to a wide range of rhythmic ideas and approaches.

Music-based workouts not only enhance the brain's cognitive functions but also contribute to the development of drumming skills through the act of active listening. During music-based workouts, drummers can tune their ears to the nuances of the music playing, focusing on the rhythms, accents, and patterns. This heightened awareness and attentiveness to the music can be transferred to their drumming practice, enabling them to better grasp the intricate rhythms and nuances in the songs they play. By training their ears through music-based workouts, drummers develop a stronger sense of rhythm, improved timing, and the ability to adapt to different musical contexts.

Furthermore, music-based workouts can also improve drummers' physical fitness, stamina, and coordination, which are crucial elements for drumming. Regular exercise enhances cardiovascular health, increases stamina, and strengthens the muscles used in drumming, resulting in improved endurance during drumming performances. The rhythmic movements and coordination required in music-based workouts also translate into improved limb independence and coordination on the drum set. The combination of physical fitness and musicality achieved through music-based workouts creates a solid foundation for drummers to excel in their craft and express themselves fully through their playing.

Music-based workouts offer a holistic approach to enhancing both the human brain and drumming skills. They provide a platform for cognitive stimulation, emotional well-being, and physical fitness, all of which are beneficial for drummers. By actively listening to music during these workouts, drummers can deepen their rhythmic understanding, develop their musicality, and improve their overall drumming skills. The combination of physical exercise, active listening, and musicality creates a synergistic effect that supports the growth and development of drummers, both as musicians and individuals.

Drumming and rhythm offer a dynamic and enjoyable way to develop coordination and motor skills. By engaging in regular drumming practice, individuals can improve motor coordination, fine motor skills, bilateral integration, and rhythm perception. The underlying mechanisms of neuroplasticity, synchronization, and cross-hemispheric communication contribute to these improvements. So, pick up those drumsticks, explore the world of rhythm, and unleash the potential for enhanced coordination and motor skills.

Chapter 3
Creating a Rhythmic Connection Through Drumming

Drumming is an ancient and universal practice that has been used by cultures across the globe for centuries. It has the power to transcend language barriers and bring people together in a profound and meaningful way. In this chapter, we will explore the art of creating a rhythmic connection through drumming, examining how it can foster unity, enhance communication, and promote personal and collective well-being.

The Power of Rhythm

Rhythm is the heartbeat of music and life itself. It is a fundamental element that permeates our existence. When we engage in drumming, we tap into this primal force and connect with something larger than ourselves. The rhythmic patterns we create have the ability to resonate within us and synchronize our bodies, minds, and souls. As we align with the beat, we enter a state of flow, where time seems to dissolve, and we become fully present in the moment.

The power of rhythm is undeniable, as it has a profound impact on our lives in various ways. Rhythm permeates our daily experiences, from the beating of our hearts to the cycles of day and night. It is a fundamental element of music, dance, and language, and it has the ability to connect us on a deep and primal level. Rhythm has the power to evoke emotions, stimulate movement, and create a sense of unity and synchronization.

In music, rhythm serves as the backbone that drives the energy and structure of a piece. It gives music its pulse, groove, and flow, inviting us to tap our feet, nod our heads, or sway our bodies in response. Rhythm has the capacity to evoke specific moods and emotions, whether it's the driving intensity of a fast-paced beat or the soothing tranquility of a slow, steady rhythm. It can uplift our spirits, inspire us to move, and even transport us to different emotional landscapes.

Beyond music, rhythm plays a vital role in our daily lives. It helps us navigate and synchronize our movements, from walking and running to typing on a keyboard or even driving a car. Rhythmic activities, such as drumming or dancing, engage our motor and sensory systems, promoting coordination, concentration, and a sense of embodiment. Rhythm has been used therapeutically to support individuals with various conditions, including Parkinson's disease, speech disorders, and trauma, as it taps into our innate ability to respond to and connect with rhythm.

Moreover, rhythm has a unifying power. It transcends cultural boundaries, language barriers, and societal divisions. Across the globe, communities have used rhythm as a means of communication, celebration, and connection for centuries. Whether it's through communal drumming circles, traditional dances, or chants, rhythm brings people together in a shared experience. It creates a sense of unity, harmony, and collective energy, fostering a deep sense of connection and belonging.

The power of rhythm is far-reaching and multifaceted. It moves us physically, emotionally, and spiritually. It has the ability to transport us, connect us, and inspire us. Rhythm is an inherent part of our human experience, and harnessing its power can bring joy, healing, and a deeper connection to ourselves and others.

Fostering Unity

Drumming circles are a perfect example of how rhythm can bring people together. In these circles, individuals of diverse backgrounds and experiences join forces to create a collective groove. Each person contributes their unique rhythms and energy to the group, forming a cohesive whole. As we drum together, we develop a sense of unity and interconnectedness, transcending our differences and celebrating our shared humanity.

Drumming and rhythm have long been recognized as powerful tools for fostering unity and promoting a sense of togetherness among individuals. Here are five ways in which drumming and rhythm contribute to unity:

1. COLLECTIVE EXPRESSION: Drumming and rhythm provide a shared platform for individuals to express themselves collectively. When people come together to drum or engage in rhythmic activities, they create a collective rhythm that transcends individual differences. Drumming enables participants to contribute their unique rhythms and sounds, creating a harmonious and collaborative musical experience.

This collective expression fosters a sense of unity and shared purpose, as individuals synchronize their actions and become part of something greater than themselves.

2. NON-VERBAL COMMUNICATION: Drumming and rhythm offer a powerful form of non-verbal communication. Through rhythm, participants can connect with one another on an instinctual level, transcending language barriers and cultural differences. The synchronized beats and patterns create a common language that allows individuals to interact and communicate in a way that goes beyond words. This non-verbal communication fosters a sense of understanding, empathy, and connection, promoting unity among participants.

3. SYNCOPATION AND INTERPLAY: In drumming and rhythm, syncopation and interplay are essential elements. Syncopation involves playing rhythms that accentuate offbeats and unexpected accents, creating a sense of tension and release. Interplay refers to the interaction between different rhythmic elements or drummers. These rhythmic techniques not only add complexity and excitement to the music but also require active listening, anticipation, and response. As participants engage in syncopation and interplay, they develop a heightened sense of connection and unity, working together to create a cohesive and dynamic musical experience.

4. CELEBRATION AND RITUAL: Drumming and rhythm have been integral to celebrations and rituals in various cultures throughout history. Whether it's a traditional ceremony, a community gathering, or a festive occasion, drumming and rhythm often form the rhythmic heartbeat of these events. The collective participation in rhythmic activities during celebrations and rituals fosters a sense of unity, as individuals come together to honor and commemorate shared values, traditions, and experiences. Drumming serves as a unifying force, bringing people together in a shared expression of joy, celebration, and cultural identity.

5. COLLABORATIVE LEARNING AND COOPERATION: Drumming and rhythm provide an environment for collaborative learning and cooperation. In group drumming sessions or ensembles, individuals learn to listen to one another, synchronize their rhythms, and work together to create a cohesive musical performance. This collaborative learning process encourages cooperation, mutual support, and respect among participants. Drumming becomes a shared journey of learning and growth, fostering a sense of unity as individuals work together towards a common goal.

Drumming and rhythm have the remarkable ability to foster unity among individuals. Through collective expression, non-verbal communication, syncopation and interplay, celebrations and rituals, and collaborative learning, drumming and rhythm create a space where people can connect, communicate, and cooperate. The power of drumming and rhythm lies in their capacity to transcend differences, create a shared sense of purpose, and forge deep connections among participants, promoting unity and a sense of belonging.

Enhancing Communication

Drumming provides a platform for nonverbal communication. Through our drumming, we can express our emotions, thoughts, and intentions without the need for words. In a drum circle, participants engage in a musical conversation, taking turns to play, respond, and build upon each other's rhythms. This rhythmic dialogue encourages active listening, empathy, and collaboration. It teaches us the importance of both individual expression and collective harmony, fostering a deeper understanding of ourselves and others.

Drumming and rhythm have a significant impact on enhancing

communication in various ways. Here are six ways in which drumming and rhythm contribute to improved communication:

1. **NON-VERBAL COMMUNICATION:** Drumming and rhythm provide a powerful means of non-verbal communication. Through the use of rhythmic patterns, dynamics, and accents, drummers can convey emotions, intentions, and ideas without the need for words. This non-verbal communication allows for a deeper level of expression, connecting with others on an instinctual and primal level.

2. **ACTIVE LISTENING:** Drumming and rhythm require active listening skills. As drummers engage in rhythmic dialogue or play in a group, they must listen attentively to the patterns and cues provided by their fellow musicians. This heightened sense of listening promotes active and focused attention, allowing drummers to pick up on subtle changes, respond in the moment, and engage in musical conversation.

3. **TIMING AND SYNCHRONIZATION:** Drumming and rhythm rely on precise timing and synchronization. When playing with others, drummers must align their rhythms, tempos, and accents to create a cohesive and synchronized sound. This emphasis on timing fosters an acute sense of timing and the ability to adapt and synchronize with others, leading to enhanced communication and coordination.

4. **EXPRESSING EMOTIONS:** Drumming and rhythm provide a powerful outlet for expressing emotions. Through the use of different rhythms, dynamics, and playing techniques, drummers can convey a wide range of emotions such as joy, excitement, anger, or sadness. This expressive capacity allows for a direct and immediate communication of emotions, providing a shared experience and understanding among musicians and listeners.

5. **IMPROVISATION AND CREATIVITY:** Drumming and rhythm often involve improvisation, where musicians create spontaneous rhythms and patterns. This improvisational aspect encourages creativity and experimentation. Drummers can express their unique ideas, explore different rhythmic possibilities, and contribute to a collective musical conversation. This creative expression fosters individuality while promoting communication and collaboration within the musical context.

6. CULTURAL EXCHANGE: Drumming and rhythm serve as vehicles for cultural exchange and understanding. Different cultures and traditions have unique rhythmic styles, instruments, and approaches to drumming. By engaging in cross-cultural drumming experiences, individuals have the opportunity to learn about and appreciate diverse musical traditions. This exchange of rhythmic ideas and practices promotes cultural understanding, respect, and a shared appreciation for the richness of global musical heritage.

Drumming and rhythm significantly enhance communication by providing a non-verbal language, promoting active listening, emphasizing timing and synchronization, enabling emotional expression, fostering improvisation and creativity, and facilitating cultural exchange. Whether in a musical context or a broader cultural setting, drumming and rhythm serve as powerful tools for connecting individuals, bridging language barriers, and fostering meaningful communication.

Promoting Personal and Collective Well-being

The act of drumming has numerous positive effects on our well-being. It is a powerful stress-reliever, helping to reduce anxiety and promote relaxation. The rhythmic vibrations produced by drumming also stimulate the release of endorphins, our brain's natural feel-good chemicals, which can elevate our mood and increase our overall sense of well-being. Furthermore, drumming is known to enhance focus, concentration, and mindfulness, allowing us to cultivate a state of deep presence and self-awareness.

Drumming and rhythm have a profound impact on promoting personal and collective well-being. Here are four ways in which drumming and rhythm contribute to overall well-being:

1. STRESS REDUCTION: Drumming and rhythm have been shown to reduce stress and promote relaxation. Engaging in drumming activities provides a rhythmic and repetitive motion that can induce a meditative state, helping to calm the mind and alleviate stress. The physicality of drumming also releases endorphins, the body's natural feel-good chemicals, which can improve mood and reduce anxiety.

2. EMOTIONAL RELEASE AND EXPRESSION: Drumming and rhythm provide a powerful outlet for emotional release and expression. The act of drumming allows individuals to channel and express their emotions through rhythm, beats, and dynamics. This cathartic release of emotions can help in processing and managing feelings of anger, sadness, or frustration. Drumming provides a healthy and creative way to release pent-up emotions, leading to a sense of emotional well-being and a greater sense of self-awareness.

3. SOCIAL CONNECTION AND COMMUNITY BUILDING: Drumming and rhythm have the power to bring people together, fostering social connection and community building. Drum circles and group drumming sessions provide a platform for individuals to connect, collaborate, and communicate through rhythm. The shared experience of drumming promotes a sense of belonging and unity, creating a supportive and inclusive community. The social interaction and sense of camaraderie that drumming brings can enhance social bonds, reduce feelings of isolation, and improve overall mental and emotional well-being.

4. COGNITIVE STIMULATION AND BRAIN HEALTH: Engaging in drumming and rhythm provides cognitive stimulation, promoting brain health and well-being. Drumming requires concentration, coordination, and memory recall, stimulating various regions of the brain. This cognitive engagement can improve focus, attention, and mental agility. Furthermore, studies have shown that drumming can enhance neuroplasticity, the brain's ability to reorganize and form new connections. Regular drumming practice has been linked to improved cognitive function, memory, and overall brain health.

Drumming and rhythm contribute to personal and collective well-being by reducing stress, facilitating emotional release and expression, promoting social connection and community building, and stimulating cognitive function. The rhythmic nature of drumming provides a powerful means of self-expression, relaxation, and social interaction. Whether engaging in individual practice or participating in group drumming activities, drumming and rhythm have a transformative effect on overall well-being, nurturing physical, emotional, and cognitive health.

Building Resilience and Empowerment

Drumming can be an empowering tool for personal growth and resilience. Through regular practice, we develop discipline, perseverance, and a stronger connection to our innate creative abilities. Drumming encourages us to step out of our comfort zones, experiment with new rhythms, and embrace the joy of improvisation. As we gain confidence in our drumming skills, we can transfer this newfound sense of empowerment to other areas of our lives, facing challenges with resilience and determination.

Drumming and rhythm play a significant role in building resilience and empowerment. Here are three ways in which drumming and rhythm contribute to these aspects:

1. **RESILIENCE THROUGH RHYTHM:** Drumming and rhythm provide a powerful avenue for building resilience. The rhythmic nature of drumming promotes a sense of stability and predictability, which can be particularly beneficial during challenging times. Drumming requires focus, discipline, and perseverance, fostering resilience by developing the ability to adapt, overcome obstacles, and maintain a steady rhythm even in the face of adversity. Engaging in drumming practices can help individuals build emotional and mental resilience, enhancing their ability to cope with stress, bounce back from setbacks, and maintain a positive outlook.

2. **EMPOWERMENT THROUGH SELF-EXPRESSION:** Drumming and rhythm empower individuals to express themselves freely and authentically. Through drumming, individuals can unleash their creativity, channel their emotions, and find their unique voice. Drumming provides a platform for self-expression and personal empowerment, allowing individuals to explore their inner rhythm and connect with their innate power. The act of drumming can be a transformative experience, empowering individuals to embrace their strengths, express their truth, and build self-confidence.

3. **COLLECTIVE EMPOWERMENT AND CONNECTION:** Drumming and rhythm also foster collective empowerment and connection. When individuals come together to drum as a group, they experience a sense of collective power and unity. The synchronized rhythms and shared energy create a supportive and empowering environment, where participants can uplift and inspire one another.

Drum circles and group drumming sessions promote a sense of belonging, cooperation, and shared purpose, empowering individuals to collaborate and create something greater than themselves. Through collective drumming, individuals build a sense of empowerment as they contribute to the collective rhythm and experience the transformative power of rhythm together.

Drumming and rhythm contribute to building resilience and empowerment by providing stability, fostering self-expression, and promoting collective empowerment and connection. Through rhythmic practices, individuals can develop resilience by embracing the steady rhythm, adapting to challenges, and maintaining a positive mindset. Drumming also empowers individuals to express themselves authentically, explore their inner rhythm, and build self-confidence. Furthermore, the collective nature of drumming promotes a sense of unity, empowerment, and shared purpose. Together, these aspects of drumming and rhythm contribute to building resilience and empowerment at both the individual and collective levels.

Drumming is a transformative practice that has the potential to create a profound rhythmic connection among individuals and communities. By engaging in drumming circles, we can foster unity, enhance communication, and promote personal and collective well-being. Whether you are a seasoned drummer or a beginner, the power of rhythm is accessible to all. Embrace the beat, feel the pulse, and let the transformative energy of drumming guide you on a journey of connection and self-discovery.

Chapter 4
Cognitive Enhancements Through Rhythm and Drumming

Throughout human history, rhythm and drumming have played a vital role in various cultures and societies. Beyond their cultural significance, they have also been found to have profound effects on the human brain and cognitive function. In this chapter, we explore the fascinating relationship between rhythm, drumming, and cognitive enhancements. We delve into the scientific research, the mechanisms behind these effects, and the potential applications of rhythmic interventions in various domains.

The Neuroscience of Rhythm and Drumming

The human brain has an innate sensitivity to rhythm. It is wired to perceive and synchronize with rhythmic patterns, a phenomenon known as entrainment. When we listen to rhythmic music or engage in rhythmic activities like drumming, our brains exhibit synchronized neural activity. This synchronization involves various brain regions, including the auditory cortex, motor areas, and the prefrontal cortex, which is responsible for higher cognitive functions.

The neuroscience of rhythm and drumming is a fascinating field of study that explores the intricate relationship between the brain, music, and human behavior. Research has shown that rhythmic activities, such as drumming, have a profound impact on the brain and can elicit various cognitive and emotional responses. When we drum or listen to rhythmic music, our brains become engaged in a complex network of neural circuits, resulting in a range of neurological effects.

One of the key findings in this area of research is the role of rhythm in promoting synchronization and coordination within the brain. When we drum, the auditory and motor regions of the brain are activated, creating a dynamic interplay between perception and action. This synchronization strengthens the connections between different brain areas, enhancing communication and facilitating efficient information processing. It is believed that regular engagement in rhythmic activities like drumming can improve motor skills, timing, and coordination.

Moreover, drumming has been found to have a profound impact on our emotional well-being. It activates the brain's reward centers, releasing feel-good neurotransmitters such as dopamine and endorphins. This can lead to an increase in positive emotions, stress reduction, and even pain relief. Drumming in a group setting, such as in drum circles or communal rituals, further amplifies these effects by fostering social bonding, a sense of belonging, and shared experiences.

Interestingly, studies have also revealed the therapeutic potential of rhythm and drumming in various clinical settings. It has been used as a complementary therapy for conditions like Parkinson's disease, where rhythmic cues can help alleviate motor symptoms and improve gait. Additionally, drumming has shown promising results in reducing anxiety, depression, and post-traumatic stress disorder (PTSD). The rhythmic nature of drumming can serve as a grounding technique, promoting relaxation and emotional regulation.

The neuroscience of rhythm and drumming sheds light on the profound impact of rhythmic activities on the brain. Drumming engages multiple neural networks, enhancing synchronization, coordination, and communication within the brain. It also has emotional and therapeutic benefits, boosting mood, reducing stress, and fostering social connections. As our understanding of the brain continues to evolve, further exploration of this field will undoubtedly unveil more insights into the powerful effects of rhythm and drumming on human cognition and behavior.

Enhanced Attention and Focus

One of the most significant cognitive benefits of rhythm and drumming is the enhancement of attention and focus. Engaging in rhythmic activities requires sustained attention and the ability to synchronize movements with a beat. Research has shown that regular drumming practice can improve attention span, concentration, and focus, both in children and adults. The rhythmic stimulation helps reduce distractions and promotes a state of flow, allowing individuals to immerse themselves fully in the task at hand.

The effect of drumming and rhythm on enhanced attention and focus has been a subject of interest in neuroscience and psychology. Studies have shown that engaging in rhythmic activities like drumming can have a positive impact on attentional processes. When individuals

drum or listen to rhythmic music, their brains become entrained to the beat, creating a state of focused attention. This synchronization of brain activity promotes a sense of flow and immersion in the present moment.

Furthermore, drumming requires a combination of physical coordination and mental concentration. As individuals play a rhythm, they need to maintain a steady beat while coordinating their movements. This dual demand on motor and cognitive skills challenges the brain to engage in multitasking, leading to enhanced attention and focus. Regular practice of drumming can improve these cognitive abilities over time, sharpening attentional control and concentration.

Additionally, the repetitive nature of drumming can induce a meditative-like state, often referred to as "drummer's high." This state is characterized by a deep sense of focus and absorption, where distractions fade away and attention becomes highly concentrated. This heightened state of attention can improve cognitive performance, memory encoding, and information processing. Drumming has even been used as a therapeutic intervention for individuals with attention deficit hyperactivity disorder (ADHD) to improve attention and self-regulation skills.

Drumming and rhythm have a notable impact on enhanced attention and focus. The synchronization of brain activity, the challenge of multitasking, and the meditative state induced by drumming contribute to increased attentional control and concentration. Whether in a professional setting, a musical performance, or as a therapeutic tool, the rhythmic nature of drumming can serve as a powerful catalyst for improving cognitive abilities and fostering a state of focused attention.

Memory and Learning

Rhythm and drumming also have positive effects on memory and learning processes. When we drum, we engage both hemispheres of the brain and activate multiple neural networks simultaneously. This cross-hemispheric communication strengthens the connections between brain regions, particularly those involved in memory formation and retrieval. Studies have indicated that incorporating rhythmic elements into learning activities, such as using drumming rhythms to reinforce information, can enhance memory retention and recall.

Drumming and rhythm have been found to enhance memory and learning in several ways, making them valuable tools for cognitive development. First, the rhythmic patterns and repetitive nature of drumming can help improve memory encoding. When individuals engage in drumming, they create a structured sequence of beats that can serve as a mnemonic device. This rhythmic organization facilitates the encoding of information into memory by providing a predictable and structured framework.

Moreover, drumming engages multiple sensory modalities, including auditory, tactile, and motor systems. This multisensory stimulation enhances the brain's ability to process and retain information. When individuals play drums, they receive auditory feedback through the sound produced, tactile feedback through the physical sensation of hitting the drum, and motor feedback through the movement required to play the instrument. This integration of sensory input strengthens neural connections and promotes more robust memory formation.

Furthermore, drumming in a group setting, such as in drum circles or ensemble performances, fosters social interaction and cooperation. These collective experiences not only create a rich learning environment but also enhance memory consolidation. The social aspect of drumming engages interpersonal connections and activates brain regions associated with social cognition. This social engagement and the emotional experiences associated with group drumming can further reinforce memory encoding and retrieval processes.

Lastly, research has demonstrated that rhythmic activities like drumming can improve attention and focus, which are crucial for effective learning and memory consolidation. By engaging in drumming, individuals are required to maintain a steady beat, coordinate their movements, and concentrate on the task at hand. This active engagement challenges the brain's executive functions and strengthens neural networks associated with attention and working memory, facilitating better learning outcomes.

Drumming and rhythm offer numerous benefits for memory and learning. The structured and repetitive nature of drumming aids in memory encoding, while the multisensory stimulation enhances information processing and retention. Group drumming experiences promote social interaction and cooperation, contributing to memory consolidation. Additionally, drumming improves attention and focus, key components for effective learning. Incorporating drumming and rhythm into educational settings or personal practice can be a powerful strategy to enhance memory and optimize learning potential.

Executive Functions

Executive functions refer to a set of cognitive processes that enable us to plan, organize, prioritize, and regulate our behavior effectively. Rhythm and drumming have been shown to have a positive impact on these executive functions. Regular rhythmic activities can improve working memory, cognitive flexibility, and inhibitory control. Drumming requires individuals to maintain a steady beat while simultaneously engaging in complex motor coordination, which exercises and strengthens these executive functions.

Drumming and rhythm have been found to provide significant benefits for individuals in terms of their executive functions. Executive functions refer to a set of cognitive processes that are responsible for goal-directed behavior, decision-making, impulse control, and cognitive flexibility. Here's how drumming and rhythm can help enhance these executive functions:

1. **COGNITIVE FLEXIBILITY:** Drumming requires individuals to switch between different rhythms, patterns, and beats. This constant adaptation and flexibility in drumming exercises can improve cognitive flexibility, allowing individuals to shift their attention, change strategies, and adjust their behavior according to the demands of the task. Regular drumming practice can enhance the brain's ability to switch between different mental sets and improve cognitive adaptability.

2. WORKING MEMORY: Working memory involves the ability to hold and manipulate information in mind. Drumming engages working memory as individuals need to remember and recall different rhythms, patterns, and sequences while coordinating their movements. By challenging working memory capacity, drumming can lead to improvements in this cognitive function, enhancing the ability to retain and manipulate information in real-time.

3. IMPULSE CONTROL: Drumming requires individuals to maintain a steady beat and resist the urge to deviate from the rhythm. This practice of inhibiting impulsive responses and maintaining self-control can transfer to other areas of life, improving impulse control and decision-making abilities. Drumming can serve as a form of self-regulation training, helping individuals develop discipline and restraint in their actions and behavior.

4. PLANNING AND ORGANIZATION: Drumming involves planning and organizing different rhythmic elements to create a cohesive musical piece. This process of structuring rhythms, coordinating movements, and anticipating upcoming beats can improve planning and organizational skills. Drumming requires individuals to break down complex tasks into smaller components, set goals, and create a systematic approach to achieve those goals. These skills can transfer to other areas of life, facilitating better planning and organization of daily activities and tasks.

5. ATTENTION AND FOCUS: Drumming requires sustained attention and concentration. The rhythmic nature of drumming can help individuals enter a state of flow, where they are fully absorbed in the activity and their attention becomes highly focused. Regular drumming practice can enhance attentional control, allowing individuals to sustain their focus, resist distractions, and maintain concentration for extended periods. This heightened attention and focus can have positive effects on other executive functions, such as problem-solving and decision-making.

Drumming and rhythm have beneficial effects on executive functions. They improve cognitive flexibility, working memory, impulse control, planning and organization, as well as attention and focus. By engaging in drumming activities, individuals can enhance their cognitive skills and develop a strong foundation for effective goal-directed behavior and decision-making. Whether it's through individual practice or group drumming experiences, incorporating drumming and rhythm into daily routines can be an effective strategy to support and enhance executive functions.

Emotional Regulation and Stress Reduction

Rhythmic activities, including drumming, have long been used as therapeutic interventions for emotional regulation and stress reduction. Drumming engages the limbic system, the brain's emotional center, and helps regulate emotional responses. The repetitive and predictable nature of rhythm induces a sense of relaxation and induces the release of endorphins and other feel-good neurotransmitters. Drum circles and group drumming sessions also promote social bonding, reducing feelings of isolation and improving overall well-being.

Drumming and rhythm have been recognized for their profound effects on emotional regulation and stress reduction. Here are four ways in which drumming can help in these areas:

1. **EMOTIONAL EXPRESSION:** Drumming provides a powerful outlet for emotional expression. When individuals engage in drumming, they can channel their emotions into the rhythmic patterns and beats they create. The act of hitting the drum can serve as a cathartic release, allowing individuals to express and process their emotions in a nonverbal and visceral manner. This emotional release can help reduce feelings of stress, anxiety, and frustration, promoting emotional well-being.

2. **STRESS REDUCTION:** Drumming has a calming effect on the body and mind. The repetitive nature of drumming induces a meditative state that can help reduce stress and promote relaxation. When individuals drum, their focus shifts to the rhythm and physical sensations, diverting attention from stressful thoughts and worries. Drumming also stimulates the production of endorphins and dopamine, neurotransmitters associated with pleasure and relaxation, further contributing to stress reduction.

3. **MINDFULNESS AND PRESENT-MOMENT AWARENESS:** Drumming encourages mindfulness and present-moment awareness. As individuals engage in rhythmic patterns, they become fully absorbed in

My view from the drum riser.
Sam Morrison Band - Dana Point, CA.

the experience, directing their attention to the present moment. This mindfulness practice helps individuals let go of rumination about the past or worries about the future, fostering a state of present-moment awareness. Drumming serves as a grounding technique, allowing individuals to connect with the present and cultivate a sense of calmness and balance.

4. SOCIAL CONNECTION AND SUPPORT: Drumming in a group setting, such as in drum circles or community gatherings, promotes social connection and support. The shared experience of drumming with others fosters a sense of belonging and unity. The synchronized rhythms and collective energy create a supportive environment where individuals can express themselves and connect with others on an emotional level. This social bonding can provide emotional regulation and a support system for coping with stress and challenges.

Drumming and rhythm offer significant benefits in the area of emotional regulation and stress reduction. They provide a platform for emotional expression, promote stress reduction, enhance mindfulness and present-moment awareness, and foster social connection and support. Incorporating drumming into one's routine, whether as a personal practice or within a group setting, can be an effective tool for managing emotions, reducing stress, and promoting overall emotional well-being.

Applications and Future Directions

The cognitive enhancements offered by rhythm and drumming hold great potential for various domains. In educational settings, incorporating rhythmic interventions can improve students' attention, memory, and learning outcomes. Drumming therapy can be utilized in clinical settings to aid individuals with attention deficit disorders, cognitive impairments, and emotional disorders. Additionally, rhythm-based interventions could be integrated into workplace environments to enhance productivity, focus, and stress management.

Drumming and rhythm have a wide range of applications and hold promising potential for future directions. Here are three areas where drumming can be beneficial:

1. **THERAPEUTIC APPLICATIONS:** Drumming has been increasingly used in therapeutic settings. Music therapists utilize drumming as a therapeutic intervention for individuals with various conditions, including autism spectrum disorder, dementia, and mental health disorders. Drumming therapy can improve cognitive skills, promote emotional expression and regulation, enhance social interactions, and contribute to overall well-being. As research in this area continues to evolve, drumming may find further applications in clinical settings, rehabilitation programs, and holistic approaches to wellness.

2. **COGNITIVE ENHANCEMENT AND LEARNING:** Drumming's impact on cognitive functions and learning has opened avenues for its application in educational settings. Incorporating drumming activities into schools and classrooms can promote attention, working memory, cognitive flexibility, and problem-solving skills. Drumming-based interventions may also support individuals with learning disabilities or attention deficit disorders. Exploring the use of drumming as a tool for cognitive enhancement and educational interventions holds promise for improving learning outcomes and academic performance.

3. STRESS MANAGEMENT AND WORKPLACE WELLNESS: The stress-reducing and relaxation effects of drumming make it a potential tool for stress management in various settings, including the workplace. Drumming sessions or workshops can serve as a means to alleviate work-related stress, boost employee well-being, and enhance team cohesion. Companies and organizations are increasingly recognizing the value of incorporating activities like drumming into their wellness programs to reduce stress, increase productivity, and improve overall work environment and employee satisfaction.

Looking ahead, future directions for drumming and rhythm research may involve exploring its effects on specific populations, such as children, older adults, and individuals with neurological conditions. Investigating the underlying neural mechanisms of drumming and its impact on brain plasticity can provide valuable insights. Additionally, advancements in technology, such as virtual reality or biofeedback systems, may offer innovative ways to incorporate drumming into therapeutic interventions or educational programs. Continued research and exploration of drumming's applications will likely uncover even more possibilities for its use in various domains of human life.

Rhythm and drumming have the power to enhance cognitive function and promote overall well-being. Whether it's through improving attention and focus, enhancing memory and learning, strengthening executive functions, or facilitating emotional regulation, the effects of rhythm on the brain are remarkable. As we continue to explore the neural mechanisms behind these cognitive enhancements, we open up exciting opportunities for leveraging rhythm and drumming in various contexts, from education and therapy to personal development and workplace productivity.

Chapter 5
Building Social Connections and Teamwork Through Drums and Rhythm

In a world where social connections are becoming increasingly digital and superficial, the need for genuine human interaction and teamwork has never been more important. Music, particularly drumming and rhythm, provides a powerful medium for fostering social connections and building effective teams. This chapter explores how drumming and rhythm can be used as a transformative tool to enhance social interactions, promote collaboration, and strengthen teamwork.

Rhythm is an inherent part of human life. It is the beating of our hearts, the rhythm of our breath, and the cadence of our footsteps. When we engage with rhythm, whether through drumming or other forms of music, something remarkable happens. We tap into a primal and universal language that transcends cultural barriers and enables us to connect on a deeper level. Rhythm has the ability to synchronize individuals, align their energies, and create a shared experience.

Drumming as a Social Activity

Drumming has been an integral part of human culture for centuries, serving as a means of communication, celebration, and unity. When people come together to drum, they enter into a collective experience that fosters social connections. In a drumming circle, individuals contribute their unique rhythms and beats, creating a vibrant tapestry of sound. As participants listen to each other and respond, a sense of harmony and camaraderie emerges.

Drumming has long been recognized as a powerful social activity that brings people together in a unique and rhythmic way. Whether it's a drum circle, a band rehearsal, or a community event, drumming creates a sense of unity and connection among participants. When people come together to drum, they not only create music, but they also form a bond that transcends language and cultural barriers. Drumming allows individuals to express themselves creatively while also listening and

Tommy Aldridge with Bart Robley

responding to others, fostering a collaborative and inclusive environment.

One of the remarkable aspects of drumming as a social activity is its ability to break down barriers and promote communication. Drumming is a universal language that can be understood by people from various backgrounds and cultures. Regardless of age, gender, or musical experience, anyone can participate in drumming and contribute to the collective rhythm. This inclusivity encourages interaction and collaboration, allowing individuals to connect on a deeper level beyond words. By drumming together, people develop a shared sense of purpose and develop empathy and understanding for one another.

Moreover, drumming as a social activity promotes a sense of well-being and emotional release. The act of drumming stimulates the release of endorphins, which are natural mood enhancers. When people drum together, they experience a collective energy that uplifts their spirits and creates a positive atmosphere. Drumming also provides a cathartic outlet for emotional expression, allowing individuals to channel their feelings and release stress or tension. The rhythmic patterns and vibrations produced by drumming can have a calming effect on the mind and body, promoting relaxation and mindfulness.

Drumming serves as a remarkable social activity that unites people, transcending cultural barriers and fostering connection and communication. It promotes inclusivity and collaboration, allowing individuals to express themselves creatively and interact with others in a meaningful way. Beyond the social aspect, drumming also contributes to emotional well-being, providing a platform for emotional release and promoting a positive and relaxed state of mind. Whether it's in a drum circle, a band, or a community gathering, drumming has the power to bring people together and create lasting bonds.

Building Trust and Communication

Drumming requires active listening and a keen sense of timing. When individuals drum together, they learn to trust each other's rhythms and cues. They must communicate non-verbally, through eye contact, body language, and the ebb and flow of their playing. These interactions foster empathy, cooperation, and mutual respect. As participants become attuned to each other's rhythms, they develop a heightened sensitivity to the needs and contributions of their teammates.

Drumming and rhythm play a vital role in building musical trust and communication among musicians. When drummers and other instrumentalists come together, they rely on rhythm as a foundation for their musical collaboration. By synchronizing their beats and following the pulse of the rhythm, they establish a sense of trust and cohesion. Drummers serve as the backbone of the ensemble, providing a steady and reliable rhythmic foundation that allows other musicians to build upon. This interdependence fosters a deep level of communication, as each musician listens and responds to the rhythm, creating a cohesive musical conversation.

In addition to establishing trust, drumming and rhythm also enhance communication among musicians by developing a heightened sense of listening and responsiveness. Drummers must pay close attention to the nuances of the rhythm and the dynamics of the ensemble. They must be attuned to the subtle changes and cues from their fellow musicians, adapting their playing accordingly. This heightened awareness promotes active listening and encourages a greater sensitivity to the musical context. Through rhythm, musicians learn to communicate non-verbally, anticipating each other's musical intentions and making instantaneous adjustments, resulting in a seamless and harmonious musical performance.

Furthermore, drumming and rhythm provide a platform for improvisation and musical exploration, allowing musicians to communicate and express themselves in a spontaneous and collaborative manner. Within the framework of rhythm, musicians can experiment with different patterns, textures, and musical ideas. Drummers, in particular, have the freedom to vary their rhythms and incorporate improvisational elements, which inspires other musicians to respond and interact creatively. This process of musical dialogue and exchange nurtures a deep sense of trust, as musicians feel supported and encouraged to take risks and explore new musical territories.

Drumming and rhythm are essential elements in building musical trust and communication among musicians. They establish a foundation of trust and cohesion, enabling musicians to collaborate effectively. Through rhythm, musicians develop a heightened sense of listening and responsiveness, enhancing their ability to communicate non-verbally. Drumming and rhythm also promote improvisation and musical exploration, fostering a creative and collaborative environment. Ultimately, the shared experience of drumming and rhythm creates a powerful musical bond, uniting musicians in a harmonious and expressive musical conversation.

Enhancing Collaboration and Creativity

Drumming circles provide an ideal environment for team building and fostering collaboration. When individuals come together with a common goal of creating music, they must find ways to work together and combine their unique skills. Each participant brings their own creative ideas and improvisations to the group, adding depth and complexity to the overall sound. Through this collaborative process, teams learn to value diversity, embrace different perspectives, and leverage individual strengths to achieve a collective vision.

Rhythm and drumming have a profound impact on enhancing collaboration and creativity among individuals. When people engage in rhythmic activities together, such as drum circles or jam sessions, they create a space for collaboration where ideas can flow freely. The shared experience of playing in sync with others fosters a sense of unity and encourages participants to listen, respond, and build upon each other's contributions. Through this collaborative process, individuals learn to trust and rely on one another, leading to a collective creative energy that fuels innovation and exploration.

Drumming and rhythm also provide a platform for creative expression. The repetitive patterns and beats of drumming create a solid framework upon which individuals can experiment and improvise. As drummers and musicians explore different rhythms, they tap into their own creative instincts and discover new ways to express themselves musically. This freedom of expression promotes individuality within a collaborative context, allowing each participant to contribute their unique ideas and styles. Through this interplay of creativity, participants inspire and influence one another, resulting in a rich and dynamic musical tapestry.

Moreover, drumming and rhythm serve as a powerful tool for breaking down barriers and encouraging open-mindedness. Regardless of musical backgrounds or skill levels, anyone can participate in drumming and contribute to the collective rhythm. This inclusivity fosters a sense of acceptance and encourages individuals to embrace diversity. As participants learn to appreciate and respect different styles and approaches, they become more open to new ideas and perspectives. This openness stimulates creativity, as individuals are exposed to a variety of influences and are inspired to think outside the box.

The immersive and embodied nature of drumming and rhythm enhances collaboration and creativity. Drumming involves physical engagement, requiring participants to use their whole bodies to produce sound and connect with the rhythm. This physicality creates a sense of presence and mindfulness, drawing individuals into the present moment and fostering a deeper connection with themselves and others. As participants synchronize their movements and energies, they establish a shared rhythm that goes beyond verbal communication. This non-verbal connection strengthens collaboration and enables individuals to tap into their intuitive and instinctive creative capacities.

Rhythm and drumming offer a powerful platform for enhancing collaboration and creativity as individuals and as in a group increment. By fostering a sense of unity and trust, drumming encourages participants to collaborate and build upon each other's ideas. It provides a space for creative expression and exploration, allowing individuals to tap into their unique artistic voices. Drumming also promotes openness and acceptance, breaking down barriers and inspiring new perspectives. Finally, the physical and embodied nature of drumming deepens the

connection among participants, facilitating non-verbal communication and unlocking intuitive creativity.

Promoting Emotional Well-being

Drumming and rhythm have a profound impact on our emotional well-being. The act of drumming releases endorphins, reduces stress, and promotes relaxation. As participants engage in rhythmic patterns, they enter a state of flow where their worries and anxieties fade away. Drumming also provides an outlet for self-expression and emotional release. Individuals can channel their emotions into the rhythm, allowing them to connect with their own feelings and connect with others at a deeper level.

Engaging in drumming activities provides an outlet for emotional expression and release. The act of drumming stimulates the release of endorphins, the body's natural mood-enhancing chemicals, which can help reduce stress and anxiety. The rhythmic patterns and vibrations produced by drumming have a soothing effect on the mind and body, promoting relaxation and a sense of calm.

Furthermore, drumming serves as a form of catharsis, allowing individuals to channel their emotions and release pent-up feelings. The physicality of drumming, as well as the rhythmic and repetitive nature of the activity, can help individuals release tension and frustration. The act of hitting the drum and creating powerful beats can serve as a healthy and constructive way to process and express emotions such as anger, sadness, or grief. Drumming provides a safe space for individuals to let go of negative emotions and find solace in the rhythmic flow.

Drumming in a group setting also fosters a sense of connection and belonging, which contributes to emotional well-being. Participating in drum circles or group drumming sessions allows individuals to connect with others who share a common interest and passion. The collective experience of drumming creates a sense of unity and camaraderie, reducing feelings of isolation and promoting a sense of belonging. This social connection can have a positive impact on emotional health by providing support, encouragement, and a sense of community.

Moreover, drumming and rhythm can help individuals develop mindfulness and improve emotional regulation. When drumming, individuals must focus their attention on the rhythm and synchronize their movements with the group. This requires being fully present in the moment, which promotes mindfulness and helps individuals let go of distracting thoughts or worries. By engaging in rhythmic activities, individuals can improve their ability to regulate their emotions, as the repetitive nature of drumming can have a calming and grounding effect, allowing them to find balance and inner peace.

Drumming and rhythm play a vital role in promoting emotional well-being. Drumming provides an outlet for emotional expression and release, stimulating the release of mood-enhancing chemicals and reducing stress. It offers a form of catharsis and allows individuals to channel and process their emotions in a healthy way. Engaging in drumming in a group setting fosters a sense of connection and belonging, while also promoting mindfulness and emotional regulation. Overall, drumming and rhythm offer a powerful means of promoting emotional well-being and nurturing a positive and balanced state of mind.

Applying Drumming to Teamwork

The lessons learned from drumming and rhythm can be applied to various team settings. Organizations and groups can incorporate drumming workshops or activities to strengthen team dynamics, foster innovation, and improve communication. Drumming can also be used in educational settings to encourage collaboration among students, develop leadership skills, and promote inclusivity.

The rhythmic nature of drumming requires individuals to listen, synchronize their actions, and work together towards a common goal. When applied to teamwork, drumming can foster a sense of unity and cooperation among team members, leading to improved communication and productivity.

Drumming encourages active listening, a crucial skill in effective teamwork. In a drumming ensemble, each participant must listen attentively to the rhythms being played by others. Similarly, in a team, actively listening to the ideas, perspectives, and concerns of colleagues is essential for understanding and finding common ground. By practicing active listening through drumming, team members can develop this skill and apply it to their collaborative efforts, ensuring that everyone's voices are heard and valued.

Drumming also promotes synchronization and coordination within a team. Just as drummers must play in sync with each other to maintain a steady rhythm, team members must align their efforts and work harmoniously towards a shared objective. The rhythmic patterns of drumming provide a tangible representation of the importance of timing and coordination. By applying this principle to teamwork, individuals can better understand the significance of their actions and how they contribute to the overall success of the team.

Drumming encourages creativity and innovation, which are valuable assets in any team setting. Drumming offers opportunities for improvisation and experimentation, allowing individuals to explore new rhythms and patterns. This creative freedom translates to teamwork by fostering an environment where team members feel empowered to think outside the box, suggest new ideas, and take calculated risks. Incorporating drumming activities into team-building exercises can stimulate creative thinking and inspire innovative approaches to problem-solving.

Drumming provides a platform for building trust and camaraderie within a team. When drummers play together, they must trust that each member will maintain the rhythm and support the collective sound. Similarly, trust is vital in a team to foster collaboration and effective decision-making. Drumming exercises can help build trust among team members by encouraging vulnerability and open communication. By participating in a shared musical experience, team members can form deeper connections and develop a sense of camaraderie that strengthens their working relationships.

Drumming can be a valuable tool for enhancing teamwork. By promoting active listening, synchronization, coordination, creativity, and trust, drumming activities can contribute to improved communication, productivity, and collaboration within a team. Drumming offers a unique and engaging way for team members to develop and strengthen their interpersonal skills, while also fostering a sense of unity and shared purpose. Whether applied in team-building exercises or incorporated into regular team activities, drumming has the potential to enhance teamwork dynamics and contribute to the overall success of a team.

Drumming and rhythm serve as powerful tools for building social connections and teamwork. Through the act of drumming together, individuals experience a shared sense of purpose, trust, and collaboration. The universality of rhythm allows people from different backgrounds and cultures to connect on a profound level, transcending language and other barriers. By incorporating drumming and rhythm into our lives, we can cultivate stronger social connections, enhance teamwork, and create a more harmonious and inclusive world.

Chapter 6
Emotional Expression and Confidence

In the realm of human emotions, music has always held a profound and transformative power. From ancient times to the present day, rhythm and drumming have played a central role in various cultures, enabling individuals to express themselves, find solace, and build confidence. This chapter explores the profound connection between emotional expression, confidence, and the rhythmic art of drumming.

Drumming as an Emotional Outlet

Drumming has long been recognized as a powerful means of emotional expression. It provides a primal and cathartic outlet for a range of emotions, allowing individuals to channel their feelings in a non-verbal and deeply visceral way. The act of striking a drum creates vibrations that resonate within us, resonating with our innermost emotions and facilitating their release.

When engaging in drumming, individuals can tap into their feelings of joy, anger, sadness, and everything in between. The rhythmic patterns created by the drums can mimic the ebb and flow of emotions, allowing for a dynamic expression of the human experience. By exploring various rhythms and intensities, drummers can convey emotions that may be difficult to articulate through words alone, providing a profound sense of release and catharsis.

Drumming has been used for centuries as an emotional outlet. Whether it's pounding out a driving beat or delicately tapping out a rhythm, drumming allows individuals to express and release their emotions in a unique and cathartic way. The physicality of drumming engages the body and mind, providing a channel for emotional energy to be channeled and transformed.

One of the primary reasons why drumming is such an effective emotional outlet is its ability to tap into primal instincts. The rhythmic patterns and beats created through drumming resonate deep within us, connecting us to our ancestral roots. This connection can be incredibly grounding and comforting, offering a sense of release and release of pent-up emotions.

Moreover, drumming allows for the release of intense emotions that may be difficult to express through words alone. It provides a non-verbal means of communication, allowing individuals to express anger, sadness, joy, or any other emotion that may be bubbling beneath the surface. Through the forceful strikes of the drums or the gentle touch of the cymbals, drummers can convey and process complex emotions that may be difficult to articulate otherwise.

Drumming can also be a form of meditation and mindfulness, providing a focused and immersive experience that helps individuals channel and release emotions. As drummers become absorbed in the rhythm and flow of their playing, they enter a state of deep concentration and presence. This meditative state allows for a release of stress and tension, as well as a heightened awareness of one's emotional state. By immersing themselves in the act of drumming, individuals can find solace, clarity, and a renewed sense of emotional balance.

Drumming serves as a powerful emotional outlet due to its ability to tap into primal instincts, offer a non-verbal means of communication, and provide a meditative and mindful experience. Whether it's pounding out aggression, expressing sadness, or celebrating joy, drumming allows individuals to connect with their emotions in a profound and transformative way. It offers a release valve for pent-up emotions, a means of self-expression, and a pathway to emotional well-being.

Confidence Building through Rhythm

Drumming not only serves as a powerful tool for emotional expression but also contributes to the development of confidence and self-assurance. When an individual begins to play the drums, they may start with hesitancy or self-doubt. However, as they practice and become more proficient, a transformation occurs.

Mastering rhythm and drumming techniques requires discipline, focus, and perseverance. As individuals gain proficiency, they begin to experience a sense of accomplishment and mastery over their instrument. This newfound skill set translates beyond the realm of music, boosting confidence and self-esteem in various aspects of life.

The act of drumming itself can also instill a sense of empowerment. As the drummer takes command of the rhythm, they become the driving force behind the music. The physicality of drumming, coupled with the sounds and vibrations it produces, create a sense of presence and impact. Drummers develop a heightened awareness of their own abilities and their ability to influence the environment around them.

Building Confidence through drumming and rhythm can be a transformative experience for individuals of all ages. Drumming provides a unique platform for personal expression and self-discovery, allowing individuals to develop a strong sense of self-confidence. Here are five ways in which drumming contributes to building confidence:

Drumming offers a tangible sense of achievement. As beginners learn basic drumming techniques and gradually progress to more complex rhythms, they experience a sense of accomplishment with each milestone reached. This progression builds confidence, as individuals witness their own growth and development as drummers. The ability to create music and rhythm with their own hands instills a sense of pride and self-assurance.

Drumming fosters a supportive and collaborative environment. In group drumming settings such as drum circles or band rehearsals, participants work together to create a cohesive rhythm. This collaborative aspect encourages individuals to contribute their unique voice to the collective sound, reinforcing a sense of belonging and confidence in their abilities. The positive feedback and encouragement from fellow drummers further boost self-esteem and confidence.

Drumming requires focus and concentration. As drummers navigate intricate patterns and syncopated rhythms, they develop a heightened sense of focus and mental agility. This ability to concentrate deeply on the task at hand translates to other areas of life, improving overall self-assurance and the belief in one's capabilities.

Furthermore, drumming serves as an outlet for self-expression and emotional release. The act of drumming allows individuals to channel their emotions and express themselves in a safe and non-judgmental space. Through the power of rhythm, drummers can communicate their feelings and experiences, promoting a sense of authenticity and self-confidence in their own voice.

Drumming provides a platform for performance and public speaking. Whether it's performing in a band, participating in drum circles, or even showcasing individual skills, drummers often find themselves in situations where they need to present their talents in front of others. Regular exposure to performing in public helps to overcome stage fright, build resilience, and cultivate confidence in one's ability to engage and captivate an audience.

Drumming and rhythm can have a profound impact on building confidence. The sense of achievement, collaboration, focus, self-expression, and performance opportunities that drumming provides contribute to personal growth and self-assurance. Whether someone is a beginner or an experienced drummer, the process of learning, playing, and sharing rhythm fosters a deep sense of confidence that transcends the drumming experience and positively influences other aspects of life.

Drum Circles and Emotional Connection

In addition to individual drumming, group drumming circles offer a unique opportunity for emotional expression and connection. Drum circles bring people together in a shared rhythmic experience, creating a sense of unity and community. Within this setting, participants have the freedom to express themselves emotionally and connect with others through the language of rhythm.

Drum circles allow individuals to let go of inhibitions and engage in a collective journey of self-expression. As participants synchronize their rhythms and contribute to the overall musical tapestry, a powerful sense of cohesion and harmony emerges. Through drumming, participants can release emotional baggage, find solace, and connect with others in a profound and non-judgmental way.

Drumming and rhythm serve as gateways to emotional expression and confidence-building. The act of drumming provides an avenue for individuals to express their innermost emotions, find catharsis, and gain a sense of release. Furthermore, drumming promotes the development of confidence, empowering individuals to overcome self-doubt and embrace their capabilities.

Drum circles have gained popularity as a powerful and transformative activity that facilitates emotional connection among participants. In a drum circle, individuals come together in a circle formation, each with their own drum or percussion instrument. Through the collective creation of rhythms and beats, drum circles provide a unique and immersive experience that promotes emotional expression and connection. Here are six ways drum circles foster emotional connection:

The other half of the rhythm section for the Sam Morrison Band; Greg Kasparian on Bass Guitar.

1. NON-VERBAL COMMUNICATION: Drum circles offer a space for non-verbal communication, allowing participants to express their emotions without the need for words. The rhythms and beats produced by each participant's drum become a form of language, conveying emotions and intentions. This non-verbal communication transcends language barriers, cultural differences, and personal backgrounds, creating a sense of unity and understanding.

2. SYNCHRONIZATION AND RESONANCE: Drum circles involve participants synchronizing their rhythms and beats with one another. As the group finds a collective groove, a powerful sense of resonance emerges. This synchronization creates a profound connection among participants, as they experience a shared rhythm and energy. The feeling of being in sync with others enhances emotional connection and fosters a sense of belonging.

3. EMOTIONAL RELEASE: Drumming in a circle provides an outlet for emotional release. Participants can tap into their emotions, whether it's joy, sadness, anger, or excitement, and channel them into their drumming. The act of hitting the drum, releasing energy and tension, can be cathartic and therapeutic. Drum circles create a safe and supportive environment where individuals can freely express and process their emotions.

4. ACTIVE LISTENING AND EMPATHY: Drum circles cultivate active listening skills, as participants tune in to the rhythms and beats produced by others. By actively listening and responding to one another, participants develop empathy and an understanding of the emotions and intentions behind each drumbeat. This active listening promotes a deep emotional connection as individuals attune to one another's rhythms and contribute to the collective musical experience.

5. MINDFULNESS AND PRESENCE: Engaging in a drum circle requires participants to be fully present in the moment. The concentration and focus required to maintain a steady rhythm facilitate a state of mindfulness. As participants become immersed in the rhythmic flow, they let go of distractions and worries, and become more attuned to their own emotions and the emotions of those around them. This mindfulness deepens the emotional connection within the circle.

6. CELEBRATION AND JOY: Drum circles often evoke a sense of celebration and joy. The collective energy generated by the group's rhythms creates an atmosphere of positivity and elation. Participants feed off this energy, experiencing a shared sense of happiness and upliftment. The joy experienced in drum circles strengthens emotional bonds among participants and fosters a sense of community.

Drum circles provide a powerful platform for emotional connection. Through non-verbal communication, synchronization, emotional release, active listening, mindfulness, and celebration, participants in drum circles experience a deep sense of connection and unity. Drumming together creates a space where emotions can be expressed, understood, and shared, fostering a profound sense of community and emotional well-being.

Whether practiced individually or in a group setting, drumming has the potential to unlock emotional depths and foster a sense of connection with oneself and others. Through rhythm, individuals can embark on a transformative journey of self-discovery and personal growth, embracing the power of music as a catalyst for emotional expression and enhanced confidence.

Chapter 7
Discipline and Time Management Through Drumming and Rhythm

Discipline and time management are essential skills that can greatly impact our personal and professional lives. While they may seem unrelated to drumming and rhythm at first glance, these elements play a significant role in the art of drumming. This chapter explores how drumming and rhythm can be powerful tools for developing discipline and enhancing time management skills. By understanding the principles of drumming and applying them to our daily lives, we can cultivate discipline, improve time management, and achieve greater success in various areas.

Section 1: The Discipline of Drumming
The Importance of Discipline

Discipline plays a crucial role in the process of learning drums and rhythm. Discipline ensures consistent practice. Learning drums and rhythm requires regular and focused practice to develop the necessary skills and techniques. It is through disciplined practice that drummers build muscle memory, coordination, and timing. Consistency in practicing fosters progress and growth, allowing drummers to improve their abilities and reach their musical goals.

Discipline enhances concentration and focus. Drumming demands a high level of concentration, as it involves coordinating multiple limbs and maintaining a steady rhythm. Through disciplined practice, drummers develop the ability to concentrate deeply on their playing, effectively shutting out distractions and maintaining focus. This heightened concentration translates to other areas of life, improving overall productivity and performance.

Discipline cultivates patience and perseverance. Learning drums and rhythm can be challenging, especially in the early stages when coordination and timing may feel difficult. It takes discipline to push through the initial hurdles and continue practicing even when progress feels slow. Drummers who embrace discipline develop patience and

Sam Morrison and crew in action.

perseverance, allowing them to overcome obstacles and achieve long-term success.

Discipline fosters a strong work ethic and self-motivation. Learning drums and rhythm requires dedication and a willingness to put in the necessary effort. Drummers who embrace discipline develop a strong work ethic, understanding the value of consistent practice and hard work. Discipline also cultivates self-motivation, as drummers take ownership of their progress and strive for continuous improvement.

Discipline is of utmost importance when learning drums and rhythm. It ensures consistent practice, enhances concentration, cultivates patience and perseverance, and fosters a strong work ethic and self-motivation. Through discipline, drummers are able to develop the necessary skills and techniques, achieve progress, and reach their musical goals. Embracing discipline as a fundamental aspect of drumming education lays the foundation for growth, mastery, and personal fulfillment in the world of rhythm and percussion.

Drumming requires discipline in various aspects, such as practice routines, technique development, and maintaining focus during performances. Without discipline, progress in drumming can be hindered, limiting the ability to express oneself musically. Learning to be disciplined in drumming can serve as a foundation for discipline in other areas of life.

Practice Routines

Drummers must establish consistent practice routines to improve their skills and maintain a high level of proficiency. Regular practice sessions help develop muscle memory, coordination, and timing. By dedicating specific time slots for practice, drummers cultivate discipline by committing to their craft and setting aside distractions.

Drumming practice routines are essential for improving skills, building technique, and maintaining progress. Here are five key aspects to consider when developing effective drumming practice routines:

1. **WARM-UP EXERCISES:** Starting each practice session with warm-up exercises is crucial for preparing the body and mind. Warm-ups may include stretching, rudimental exercises, or basic coordination drills. These exercises help to loosen up muscles, improve blood flow, and promote flexibility, setting a solid foundation for the practice session ahead.

2. **TECHNIQUE DEVELOPMENT:** Practice routines should include dedicated time for developing and refining drumming techniques. This can involve working on specific sticking patterns, hand and foot coordination exercises, or practicing rudiments. Focusing on technique helps to build precision, speed, and control, enhancing overall drumming abilities.

3. **RUDIMENTAL STUDIES:** Incorporating rudiments into practice routines is vital for developing a strong foundation in drumming. Rudiments are the fundamental patterns and combinations of drumming strokes, such as single strokes, double strokes, and paradiddles. Regular practice of rudiments helps to improve hand speed, control, and independence, providing the drummer with a wide range of vocabulary to apply in various musical contexts.

4. **MUSICAL REPERTOIRE:** Devoting time to learning and playing music is essential for drummers. Whether it's working on songs from different genres, studying drum parts of favorite bands, or improvising over musical tracks, including musical repertoire in practice routines helps to apply techniques and concepts in a musical context. This enhances musicality, groove, and the ability to play with other musicians.

5. CREATIVE EXPLORATION: Allowing time for creative exploration is important in drumming practice routines. This can involve improvisation, experimenting with different rhythms, exploring new sounds, or composing original drum parts. This creative exploration nurtures individuality, encourages self-expression, and fosters a deeper connection with the instrument.

Moreover, it's crucial to establish a practice schedule and stick to it consistently. Setting aside dedicated time for practice, even if it's just a few minutes each day, is more effective than irregular and sporadic sessions. It's also beneficial to break down practice routines into smaller, manageable segments, focusing on specific goals or areas of improvement in each session.

Drumming practice routines should include warm-up exercises, technique development, rudimental studies, musical repertoire, and creative exploration. Consistency, organization, and goal-oriented approaches are key to effective practice routines. By dedicating time to various aspects of drumming and maintaining a structured practice routine, drummers can continuously improve their skills, broaden their musical vocabulary, and reach their full potential as musicians.

Setting Goals

I can't write this section without mentioning my dear friend Chip Ritter. Chip is an amazing drummer and my "due north" when it comes to how one should set goals.

Discipline in drumming involves setting realistic and measurable goals. Whether it's mastering a new technique, learning a complex rhythm, or preparing for a performance, goal setting provides a sense of direction and motivation. Drummers can break down larger goals into smaller, manageable tasks, practicing discipline by working steadily towards their objectives.

Setting goals provides direction, motivation, and a sense of accomplishment. Here are five reasons why setting goals is crucial in the drumming journey:

1. FOCUS AND DIRECTION: Setting specific goals helps drummers maintain focus and direction in their practice. Goals provide a clear purpose and vision, guiding drummers on what they want to achieve.

Whether it's mastering a particular technique, learning a complex drum pattern, or joining a band, having well-defined goals allows drummers to structure their practice sessions and progress with purpose.

2. MOTIVATION AND DRIVE: Goals serve as powerful motivators. When drummers set goals, they create a sense of urgency and drive to work towards achieving them. The desire to accomplish a specific goal fuels dedication and commitment, pushing drummers to consistently practice and improve. As milestones are reached and goals are accomplished, the sense of achievement further boosts motivation and encourages continued growth.

3. MEASURE PROGRESS: Setting goals provides a framework for measuring progress. By breaking down larger goals into smaller, manageable steps, drummers can track their improvement over time. Regularly assessing progress not only helps drummers stay motivated but also provides valuable feedback on areas that require more attention and practice. Clear goals allow drummers to celebrate incremental achievements and witness their growth as musicians.

4. ACCOUNTABILITY AND DISCIPLINE: Goals hold drummers accountable for their progress and practice routines. When goals are set, drummers create a commitment to themselves and their development. This commitment fosters discipline, as drummers become more accountable for their time, effort, and consistency in practicing. By setting goals, drummers establish a framework that promotes consistent and focused practice, which is essential for growth and skill development.

5. PERSONAL SATISFACTION: Achieving goals in drumming brings a deep sense of personal satisfaction. When drummers set challenging goals and work hard to attain them, the feeling of accomplishment and fulfillment is incredibly rewarding. The satisfaction of seeing progress and achieving what was once considered difficult or impossible instills a sense of pride and self-confidence. This personal satisfaction becomes a driving force for continuous growth and sets the stage for setting even higher goals in the future.

Setting goals when learning drums and rhythm is crucial for

maintaining focus, motivation, and measuring progress. Goals provide a clear direction, foster discipline, and fuel personal satisfaction. By setting specific and achievable goals, drummers can stay on track, enjoy the journey of learning, and continuously improve their skills and musicality.

Focus and Concentration

Drumming requires intense focus and concentration to maintain rhythm, execute fills, and stay in sync with other musicians. Through the process of practicing focus and concentration on the drums, drummers develop a valuable skill that can be transferred to other areas of life. Improved focus enables individuals to prioritize tasks, minimize distractions, and achieve greater productivity.

Learning to play the drums can significantly improve focus and concentration skills. Playing the drums requires precise coordination of both hands and feet, which demands a high level of concentration and focus. Here are four key ways in which learning drums can enhance these cognitive abilities:

MENTAL DISCIPLINE: Playing the drums requires a great deal of mental discipline. Drummers must maintain a consistent rhythm and timing while executing complex patterns and fills. This constant mental engagement helps develop focus and concentration, as drummers must remain attentive and focused on their performance.

MULTITASKING ABILITIES: Drumming involves performing different movements simultaneously with different limbs. This multitasking aspect forces drummers to develop their ability to focus on multiple tasks at once, training their brains to manage different rhythms and patterns simultaneously. By mastering this skill, drummers can transfer their enhanced multitasking abilities to other areas of life, where the ability to focus on multiple tasks is crucial.

LISTENING SKILLS: Drummers need to have excellent listening skills to maintain a steady beat and synchronize with other musicians. They must actively listen to the music being played around them and adjust their timing accordingly. This heightened auditory focus and concentration foster the ability to tune out distractions and focus on

specific sounds or cues, which can be beneficial in various contexts. Personally I remember in one of my lessons with the great Dom Famularo he said to me "Bart, you have to learn to listen to music." This was extremely eye opening.

Improving attention span: Drumming requires sustained attention over extended periods. As drummers practice for longer durations, they train themselves to stay focused and maintain their concentration for extended periods of time. This enhanced attention span can translate into other areas of life, such as work or studying, where the ability to concentrate for extended periods is essential.

Learning drums can have a profound impact on focus and concentration. The mental discipline, multitasking abilities, improved listening skills, and increased attention span that come with playing the drums all contribute to developing and strengthening these cognitive skills. Whether it's in the practice room or in everyday life, the benefits of drumming extend beyond music, making it a valuable tool for enhancing focus and concentration.

Section 2: Time Management in Drumming Rhythmic Precision:

Drumming revolves around rhythm, which serves as a foundation for time management. A drummer's ability to maintain consistent tempo, execute precise rhythms, and stay in sync with other musicians is crucial. This attention to timing translates into an understanding of the importance of time management in daily life.

It requires a deep understanding and mastery of rhythmic precision, which in turn promotes effective time management skills. As drummers strive to maintain a steady beat and execute intricate patterns, they learn the importance of managing their time within the structure of the music. They must develop a strong sense of timing and pacing, ensuring that each note and accent aligns perfectly with the rhythm. This level of rhythmic precision instills a disciplined approach to time management, as drummers learn to allocate their time and energy efficiently to maintain a consistent tempo and flow. The ability to manage time effectively and maintain rhythmic precision on the drums can translate to other aspects of life, helping drummers become more organized, punctual, and efficient in their daily tasks and responsibilities.

Metronome as a Time Management Tool

Drummers often use a metronome—a device that provides a steady beat—to practice timing and develop a strong sense of rhythm. This tool teaches drummers to manage their time effectively within the structure of a specific tempo. By utilizing a metronome, drummers learn to pace themselves, allocate time efficiently, and maintain consistency, skills that can be transferred to managing time in various situations.

Using a metronome as a time management tool can greatly enhance one's ability to stay organized and focused. The three key benefits of incorporating a metronome into your practice routine:

1. ESTABLISHING A STEADY TEMPO: A metronome provides a consistent and reliable beat that serves as a reference point for timing. By practicing with a metronome, musicians learn to lock in their playing with the steady rhythm, improving their ability to maintain a consistent tempo. This skill carries over to other areas of life, as individuals become better at managing their time and staying on track with deadlines and schedules.

2. BUILDING DISCIPLINE AND ACCOUNTABILITY: Playing with a metronome requires discipline and accountability. Musicians must adhere to the metronome's beat and maintain synchronization, which fosters a sense of responsibility and focus. This discipline translates into effective time management skills, as individuals learn to allocate their time efficiently and prioritize tasks to meet deadlines and achieve goals.

3. ENHANCING CONCENTRATION AND FOCUS: The consistent ticking sound of a metronome can help sharpen concentration and focus during practice sessions. Musicians must pay close attention to the metronome's beat and remain mentally engaged to ensure they play in time. This heightened level of concentration carries over to other areas of life, enabling individuals to maintain focus on tasks, avoid distractions, and manage their time effectively.

Incorporating a metronome as a time management tool not only improves musicians' sense of timing and rhythm but also helps develop discipline, accountability, and concentration. These skills extend beyond the realm of music, enhancing one's ability to manage time, stay focused, and achieve goals in various aspects of life.

Tempo and Task Allocation

Drummers must adapt to different tempos and time signatures based on the musical piece they are playing. Similarly, in life, individuals encounter tasks with varying time constraints and priorities. Drumming teaches us the importance of assessing the time needed for each task, allocating resources accordingly, and maintaining a steady rhythm to accomplish goals efficiently.

Tempo, as a drummer in a band, plays a crucial role in task allocation and time management. The significance of tempo in relation to task allocation for drummers in a band:

1. SETTING THE RHYTHMIC FOUNDATION: As the drummer, your primary responsibility is to establish and maintain the rhythm and tempo of the music. Your role is to provide a solid foundation for the rest of the band to build upon. By setting an appropriate tempo, you create a framework within which other musicians can allocate their tasks and execute their parts effectively.

2. SYNCING WITH THE BAND: Drummers must synchronize with the other band members to create a cohesive sound. The tempo you establish allows the guitarist, bassist, and other instrumentalists to align their parts with the rhythm. This synchronization enables each member to allocate their tasks based on the tempo and play in harmony, resulting in a tight and well-coordinated performance.

3. TASK DISTRIBUTION WITHIN DRUMMING: Within drumming itself, tempo influences the allocation of tasks among various drum components. Different tempos may require adjustments in the allocation of patterns, fills, and accents on the different drum elements, such as the snare, bass drum, and cymbals. Adapting and allocating tasks according to the tempo allows drummers to create dynamic and engaging rhythmic patterns that complement the music being played.

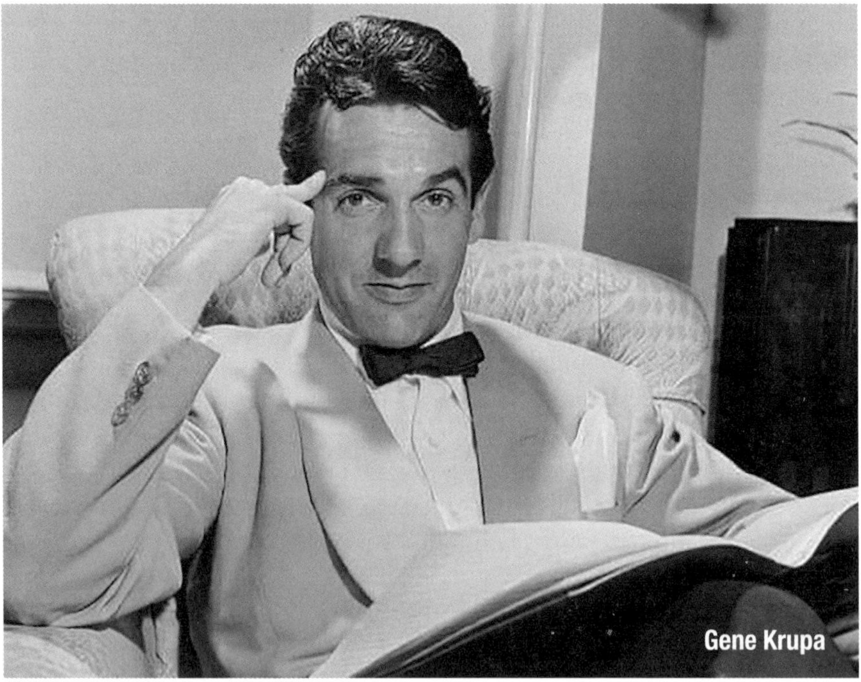
Gene Krupa

4. SUPPORTING TRANSITIONS AND DYNAMICS: Tempo changes and variations can add depth and excitement to a band's performance. As a drummer, you play a critical role in executing these transitions smoothly. Task allocation during tempo changes may involve adjusting drum patterns, fills, or shifts in intensity to match the new tempo. By effectively managing these transitions, you enhance the overall musical experience and keep the band in sync.

5. TIME MANAGEMENT DURING REHEARSALS AND PERFORMANCES: Drummers must effectively manage their time during rehearsals and performances. This includes allocating practice time to work on specific rhythmic patterns, fills, or tempo adjustments. During live performances, drummers must remain mindful of the allocated time for solos, breaks, or specific rhythm changes. Proper task allocation within the performance timeframe ensures a balanced and engaging drumming performance.

6. ADAPTING TO THE MUSIC STYLE: Different music styles have distinct tempos and rhythmic characteristics. Drummers must adapt their task allocation and playing approach accordingly. For example, in faster-paced genres like punk or metal, drummers may allocate tasks to incorporate rapid double-bass drumming or intricate fills. In slower ballads, task allocation may focus on providing a solid, laid-back groove. Adapting to the music style helps drummers allocate their tasks effectively and contribute to the overall musical expression.

Tempo plays a fundamental role in task allocation for drummers in a band. By establishing and maintaining a suitable tempo, drummers synchronize with the band, distribute tasks within drumming itself, support transitions and dynamics, and effectively manage time during rehearsals and performances. Task allocation within the tempo ensures a cohesive and engaging musical experience, showcasing the drummer's ability to adapt to different music styles and contribute to the overall band's performance.

Syncing with Others

When playing in a band or ensemble, drummers must synchronize their rhythm with other musicians. This collaborative aspect of drumming emphasizes the significance of teamwork and coordination. Applying this principle to time management, individuals learn to align their schedules and priorities with others, ensuring efficient utilization of shared time and resources.

1. **ESTABLISHING A MUSICAL CONNECTION:** Drummers serve as the rhythmic backbone of a band, providing the pulse and foundation for other musicians. Syncing with others involves developing a strong musical connection and understanding. Drummers must listen attentively to the other instruments and adjust their playing to match the overall sound and feel of the music. This connection allows for a seamless integration of different musical elements, resulting in a cohesive and harmonious performance.

2. **PRECISION AND TIMING:** As a drummer, precision and timing are paramount. Drummers must have impeccable timing to lock in with the bassist, guitarist, and other musicians. The ability to synchronize rhythms and accents precisely enhances the overall sound and energy of the band. It requires a keen sense of listening, concentration, and coordination to anticipate and respond to the musical cues and changes happening around you.

3. **COMMUNICATION AND NON-VERBAL CUES:** Syncing with others as a drummer often involves non-verbal communication. Drummers use various cues and signals, such as eye contact, body language, and subtle gestures, to communicate with other musicians during a performance. These non-verbal cues help maintain synchronization and allow for seamless transitions, tempo changes, and dynamics. Effective communication through these cues enables the band to stay in sync and adapt to each other's musical expressions, resulting in a cohesive and captivating musical experience.

Syncing with others is crucial for drummers to create a tight and cohesive sound within a band or ensemble. It requires developing a strong musical connection, precise timing, and effective communication through non-verbal cues. By mastering the art of syncing with others, drummers contribute to a unified and harmonious performance, elevating the overall musical experience for both the band members and the audience.

Drumming and rhythm serve as powerful tools for developing discipline and improving time management skills. By practicing discipline in drumming through consistent practice routines, goal setting, and focus, drummers can also transfer these skills to other areas of life.

John Bonham

Chapter 8:
Unleashing Creativity and Innovation Through Drumming and Rhythm

Throughout history, humans have used rhythm and music as a means of self-expression, communication, and celebration. Drumming, in particular, has been an integral part of cultures worldwide, serving as a powerful tool for unleashing creativity and fostering innovation. In this chapter, we will explore the profound connection between drumming, rhythm, and the enhancement of creative thinking processes. We will delve into the neurological and psychological mechanisms behind this phenomenon and explore practical ways in which drumming can be utilized to unlock the boundless potential of creativity and innovation.

The Power of Rhythm

Rhythm is an inherent part of our existence. From the steady beat of our hearts to the cyclical patterns found in nature, rhythm permeates every aspect of our lives. It is no wonder that engaging with rhythm through drumming can have a profound impact on our cognitive processes. When we drum, we synchronize our minds and bodies with a rhythmic pattern, resulting in a state of flow where our thoughts, emotions, and physical actions merge into a harmonious whole.

The power of rhythm extends beyond its musical applications and has the potential to fuel creativity and innovation. Rhythm provides a structured framework that engages our brains and bodies in a synchronized and repetitive pattern. This entrainment of rhythm stimulates our neural pathways, enhancing cognitive processes and fostering a conducive environment for creative thinking. The inherent predictability and repetition of rhythm create a sense of order and stability, allowing our minds to explore novel ideas within a structured framework. Moreover, rhythm has the power to evoke emotions and inspire movement, unlocking a deeper level of expression and opening the doors to innovative thinking. By harnessing the power of rhythm, individuals can tap into their creative potential and foster a culture of innovation in various domains beyond music.

Enhancing Brain Function

Numerous studies have shown that drumming can stimulate brain activity and enhance cognitive functions. When we engage in rhythmic activities, such as drumming, various regions of the brain are activated, including those responsible for motor coordination, sensory processing, and emotional regulation. The rhythmic stimulation triggers the release of endorphins and dopamine, promoting a sense of pleasure and reward, while simultaneously reducing stress and anxiety. This neurochemical response creates an optimal environment for creativity and innovation to flourish.

Rhythm has the remarkable ability to enhance brain function in several ways.

1. COGNITIVE COORDINATION: Engaging with rhythm activates multiple areas of the brain, promoting cognitive coordination and integration. When we listen to or play rhythmic patterns, various brain regions responsible for auditory processing, motor coordination, and attention are stimulated simultaneously. This synchronized activation strengthens the connections between these regions, improving overall cognitive coordination. As a result, individuals can enhance their ability to process information, coordinate movements, and sustain focused attention.

2. MEMORY AND LEARNING: Rhythm has a profound impact on memory and learning processes. Research suggests that rhythmic patterns and beats can enhance memory recall and information retention. The repetitive nature of rhythm creates a predictable structure that the brain can encode and store more effectively. Moreover, rhythmic activities such as drumming or clapping can improve the brain's ability to synchronize and process information, leading to enhanced learning and memory consolidation. Utilizing rhythm-based techniques in educational settings or while studying can therefore optimize the brain's capacity to absorb and retain information.

3. EMOTIONAL WELL-BEING AND STRESS REDUCTION: Rhythm has a direct influence on our emotions and can contribute to reducing stress and promoting emotional well-being. The repetitive and structured nature of rhythm induces a calming effect on the brain,

activating the parasympathetic nervous system and reducing the production of stress hormones. Engaging with rhythmic activities, such as drumming or dancing, can increase the release of endorphins and dopamine, which are associated with positive emotions and feelings of pleasure. This emotional regulation facilitated by rhythm can contribute to improved mental health, stress management, and overall well-being.

Rhythm offers a multitude of benefits for brain function. It enhances cognitive coordination, improves memory and learning processes, and contributes to emotional well-being and stress reduction. By incorporating rhythmic activities into daily routines, individuals can tap into the power of rhythm to optimize their brain function, boost cognitive abilities, and promote a healthier and more balanced mind.

Unlocking Creativity

Drumming provides a unique platform for self-expression, allowing individuals to tap into their innate creativity. The act of drumming frees the mind from the constraints of linear thinking and encourages a more fluid and intuitive approach to problem-solving. By embracing rhythm, individuals can break through mental barriers, access their subconscious mind, and discover novel solutions to challenges.

Drummers, percussionists, and musicians in general can explore new creative avenues by diving deeper into rhythm and drumming. They can experiment with different beats, patterns, and improvisations, pushing the boundaries of their musical expression. Drumming can inspire unique rhythms and textures that fuel their creative process and lead to innovative compositions or performances.

Drumming and rhythm can also be a powerful tool for artists and writers seeking inspiration. Engaging in drumming sessions or rhythmic exercises can stimulate their senses, awaken their imagination, and unlock new creative ideas. The rhythmic patterns and vibrations can inspire visual artists to experiment with shapes, colors, and textures, while writers may find rhythm as a metaphor or structure to infuse into their writing.

Even individuals who are not musicians can benefit from drumming and rhythm as a means to unlock their creativity. Drum circles, for example, provide a communal space where people can gather to explore rhythm, connect with others, and tap into their innate creative energy. Engaging in group drumming activities or rhythmic exercises can inspire fresh perspectives, encourage self-expression, and provide a sense of freedom and release. This can be particularly beneficial for individuals seeking alternative ways to express their creativity beyond traditional artistic mediums.

Anyone with an interest in exploring rhythm and drumming can unlock their creativity through these practices. Whether they are musicians, artists, writers, or non-musicians, drumming and rhythm offer a platform for self-expression, inspiration, and creative exploration. By embracing the power of rhythm, individuals can tap into their innate creativity and discover new avenues of expression and innovation.

Collaborative Drumming and Innovation

Drumming is not limited to an individual endeavor. It has a remarkable ability to bring people together, fostering collaboration and innovation. When individuals participate in group drumming sessions, they form a collective rhythm that transcends individuality, creating a shared experience of unity and interconnectedness. This collaborative aspect of drumming mirrors the dynamics of successful innovative teams, where diverse perspectives and ideas converge to generate breakthrough solutions.

Collaborative drumming can be a catalyst for innovation by fostering teamwork, communication, and creative problem-solving. When drummers come together to create music as a team, they engage in a dynamic exchange of ideas and rhythms. Each drummer brings their unique style and perspective to the collaboration, creating a diverse blend of sounds and patterns. Through active listening and responding to one another's rhythms, drummers develop a heightened sense of collaboration, adaptability, and open-mindedness. This collaborative approach encourages innovative thinking as they experiment with different combinations, explore new rhythmic possibilities, and create music that pushes the boundaries of traditional drumming.

Collaborative drumming promotes innovation through the exploration of different musical genres and cultural influences. By incorporating diverse rhythms and techniques from various musical traditions, drummers expand their creative horizons and challenge conventional norms. This cross-pollination of ideas and styles can lead to the development of unique and innovative rhythmic patterns. Collaborative drumming encourages participants to step outside their comfort zones, embrace cultural diversity, and combine elements from different genres to create fresh and innovative sounds. It fosters a spirit of experimentation and risk-taking, which are essential components of the creative process and can spark groundbreaking ideas and approaches to drumming and music as a whole.

Applied Drumming in Creative Processes

Drumming can be integrated into various creative processes to unleash innovation across different domains. Here are a few practical applications:

1. **BRAINSTORMING SESSIONS:** Incorporate short drumming sessions to kickstart brainstorming sessions. The rhythmic engagement will energize participants, promote relaxation, and stimulate divergent thinking, leading to the generation of unique ideas.

2. **IMPROVISATION AND JAMMING:** Encourage creative exploration through improvisational drumming sessions. This allows individuals to tap into their intuition, take risks, and embrace the unknown. The collaborative aspect of jamming cultivates an environment of trust and openness, where ideas can flow freely.

3. **DESIGN THINKING WORKSHOPS:** Integrate drumming exercises during design thinking workshops to enhance empathy, encourage active listening, and foster a sense of collective purpose. The rhythmic patterns can mirror the iterative nature of the design process, promoting adaptability and resilience.

4. **TEAM-BUILDING ACTIVITIES:** Utilize drumming as a team-building tool to strengthen communication, coordination, and trust within teams. Group drumming sessions can break down barriers, encourage active listening, and promote a sense of camaraderie, leading to enhanced collaboration and innovation.

Drumming and rhythm provide a gateway to unlock the immense power of creativity and innovation. Through the synchronization of mind, body, and rhythm, individuals can tap and innovation in profound ways.

Drumming and engaging with rhythm offers a unique avenue for self-expression, exploration, and collaboration. It transcends cultural boundaries and connects people at a primal level, bypassing language and facilitating a universal language of rhythm. Whether it is through the precision and coordination required to play complex patterns or the improvisational freedom to explore new beats, drumming ignites the imagination and fuels the creative spirit. By embracing the power of drumming and rhythm, individuals can unlock a world of endless possibilities, where innovation thrives and the boundaries of creativity are constantly pushed. It is a gateway that invites us to embark on a transformative journey of self-discovery, unleashing the immense power within us to create and innovate through the rhythmic language of the drums.

Chapter 9
Lifelong Learning and a Musical Journey Through Drumming and Rhythm

Lifelong learning is a transformative journey that enriches our lives, expands our horizons, and keeps our minds vibrant. It is a commitment to continuous growth, exploration, and acquiring new skills. In this chapter, we embark on a musical journey through the world of drumming and rhythm, exploring how it serves as a powerful vehicle for lifelong learning.

Drumming and rhythm is a deeply rewarding and fulfilling journey. Whether you are a beginner or an experienced drummer, there is always something new to discover and explore within this art form. As we've learned drumming requires a combination of physical coordination, mental focus, and a keen sense of timing, making it an excellent activity for brain development and cognitive skills. As you progress in your drumming journey, you will continuously encounter new rhythms, techniques, and styles from various musical genres, expanding your musical vocabulary and enhancing your rhythmic sensibilities.

One of the most exciting aspects of lifelong learning in drumming is the opportunity for self-expression and creativity. As you gain proficiency, you can experiment with different rhythms, fills, and improvisations, allowing you to develop your unique drumming style. The constant exploration of rhythm and its application to different musical contexts enables you to become a versatile musician. Moreover, drumming is a communal activity, and engaging with other musicians in jam sessions, bands, or orchestras provides endless opportunities for collaboration and growth. Lifelong learning in drumming not only improves your musical skills but also promotes discipline, perseverance, and a sense of accomplishment, fostering personal development and a lifelong passion for music.

The great Charlie Watts, (founding drummer of The Rolling Stones) once said, "It's been years and years and years I've been playing the drums, and they're still a challenge."

The Rhythm of Life

Rhythm is an inherent part of our existence. From the beating of our hearts to the cadence of our breath, rhythm permeates every aspect of our lives. It connects us to our primal instincts and serves as a universal language that transcends cultural and linguistic barriers.

The Universality of Rhythm

Rhythm is an inherent and universal element of human expression, transcending cultural boundaries and connecting people across the globe. From the beating of our hearts to the patterns of our breath, rhythm permeates every aspect of our existence. It is not limited to music alone but extends to language, movement, and even the cadence of our daily routines. The universality of rhythm speaks to its fundamental role in human communication, culture, and our shared human experience.

Across different cultures and musical traditions, rhythm serves as a common thread that weaves together diverse communities. Whether it is the intricate polyrhythms of West African drumming, the syncopated grooves of Latin American salsa, or the complex time signatures found in Indian classical music, rhythm plays a central role in shaping cultural identities and fostering a sense of belonging. The power of rhythm lies in its ability to evoke emotions, unite people in celebration or mourning, and provide a framework for collective expression.

Moreover, rhythm serves as a means of communication that surpasses language barriers. The pulsating beats and rhythmic patterns found in music allow us to connect with others on a deeper level, transcending linguistic limitations. Rhythm has the ability to convey messages, emotions, and stories that resonate with individuals across cultures and languages. It is through rhythm that we find a universal language, a shared understanding that transcends the boundaries of words and allows us to connect with one another in a profound and meaningful way.

The universality of rhythm also extends beyond music, permeating other aspects of our lives. From the rhythm of our footsteps to the rhythm of our speech, we instinctively incorporate rhythm into our daily routines. We synchronize our movements when we dance, march, or engage in physical activities, creating a sense of unity and harmony. Rhythm influences our perception of time, guiding our sense of pace, and providing structure to our experiences. It is through rhythm that we find a natural order in the chaos of life, allowing us to navigate and make sense of the world around us.

The universality of rhythm highlights its essential role in human expression and communication. It serves as a powerful force that transcends cultural boundaries, connecting individuals and communities around the world. Whether in music, language, or everyday life, rhythm unites us, allowing us to communicate, connect, and celebrate our shared humanity. Embracing the universality of rhythm not only deepens our understanding of different cultures but also reinforces our common bonds, fostering empathy, and promoting harmony in an increasingly diverse and interconnected world.

Drumming as an Expression

Drumming has been an integral part of human culture for centuries, serving as a means of communication, celebration, and ritual. It allows us to express emotions, connect with others, and tap into our creativity. The act of drumming engages our entire being—mind, body, and spirit—and fosters a deep sense of presence and mindfulness.

Drumming is a powerful form of expression that transcends language and cultural barriers. Through the rhythmic beats and percussive sounds, drumming allows individuals to communicate and convey emotions in a unique and profound way. Whether it is the thunderous beats of rock music, the intricate polyrhythms of African drumming, or the pulsating rhythms of Latin percussion, drumming serves as a universal language that speaks to the depths of human emotion.

At its core, drumming is a physical and visceral experience. The act of striking the drumheads and cymbals with hands or sticks creates a direct connection between the drummer and the instrument. This physicality enables drummers to channel their emotions and release their energy through the power of rhythm. The pounding of the drums can express anger, frustration, or aggression, while the gentle taps and soft strokes can convey tranquility, longing, or melancholy. Drumming becomes a cathartic outlet, allowing individuals to release and express their innermost feelings.

Drumming is also a means of personal and cultural identity. Each drummer brings their own unique style and personality to their playing, resulting in a distinct expression of self. Whether it is the improvisational skills of a jazz drummer, the syncopated grooves of a funk drummer, or the technical virtuosity of a metal drummer, the individuality of drumming allows musicians to express their artistic voice and showcase their creativity. Moreover, drumming is deeply rooted in various cultural traditions and plays a crucial role in cultural expression and heritage. From tribal drumming ceremonies to ceremonial rituals and celebrations, drumming serves as a vital element in preserving and transmitting cultural identity from one generation to another.

As we've learned drumming is also a form of communication and connection with others. In collaborative musical settings, drummers interact with fellow musicians to create a cohesive and dynamic sound. The interplay of rhythms and grooves establishes a musical conversation, where drummers respond and complement each other's playing. Drum circles and group drumming sessions bring people together, fostering a sense of unity and community. In these communal settings, drumming becomes a shared expression, promoting cooperation, and strengthening social bonds.

Drumming goes beyond the realm of music. It has found its way into therapeutic practices, providing a means of emotional and physical healing. Drum therapy and drumming circles are used to reduce stress, promote relaxation, and enhance overall well-being. The rhythmic patterns and vibrations produced by drumming have a profound impact on the human body, activating different parts of the brain and stimulating sensory and motor functions. Through drumming, individuals can release tension, find inner peace, and achieve a sense of balance and harmony.

Drumming is a captivating and multifaceted form of expression. It allows individuals to communicate their emotions, celebrate cultural identity, connect with others, and promote personal and collective well-being. Drumming transcends boundaries, speaking a universal language that resonates with people across cultures and languages. Whether as a form of artistic expression, cultural preservation, or therapeutic practice, drumming holds immense power in its ability to convey the depths of human emotion and bring people together in a rhythmic harmony.

Ginger Baker

Cognitive Benefits

Learning to play drums stimulates the brain in numerous ways. It enhances cognitive functions such as memory, attention, and coordination. The complex patterns and rhythms involved in drumming activate different regions of the brain, promoting neural plasticity and strengthening connections between various areas.

The Cognitive Benefits of Lifelong Learning of Rhythm and Drumming

Engaging in a lifelong journey of learning of rhythm and drumming offers numerous cognitive benefits that go beyond the realm of music. As we've learned a complex and multi-dimensional activity, drumming requires coordination, concentration, and the ability to synchronize with others. This process stimulates various cognitive functions and enhances brain development, making it a valuable pursuit for individuals of all ages.

Rhythm and drumming have a positive impact on memory and attention. Learning and playing different rhythmic patterns on drums necessitate focused attention and the ability to remember and reproduce specific sequences. This continuous mental exercise strengthens neural connections, improving working memory and concentration skills. Moreover, drumming engages both the left and right hemispheres of the brain, promoting hemispheric communication and enhancing overall cognitive functioning.

Furthermore, drumming promotes motor skills development. Coordinating different drumming techniques, such as using hands and feet simultaneously, challenges the brain to send precise signals to different body parts. This coordination fosters fine motor control, dexterity, and spatial awareness. Research has shown that regular drumming practice can lead to improved hand-eye coordination, motor planning, and overall physical coordination.

In addition to motor skills, rhythm and drumming also have a positive impact on language and communication abilities. The rhythmic patterns and timing inherent in drumming mirror the patterns and timing of speech. Regular exposure to rhythm and drumming can enhance auditory processing and timing skills, which are crucial for speech and language development. Drumming also provides a platform for non-verbal communication, as individuals can express emotions, intentions, and ideas through rhythmic patterns and dynamics, promoting a deeper understanding and connection with others.

Moreover, lifelong learning of rhythm and drumming fosters creativity and problem-solving skills. Drumming encourages individuals to think outside the box, experiment with different rhythms, and explore new patterns and sounds. This process stimulates the brain's creative centers and enhances divergent thinking. Drumming also requires problem-solving skills, as musicians must adapt to different musical contexts, adjust to changes in tempo or dynamics, and collaborate with other musicians. These cognitive demands foster adaptability, flexibility, and critical thinking.

Another cognitive benefit of lifelong learning of rhythm and drumming is stress reduction and emotional well-being. Engaging in drumming can serve as a form of active meditation, providing a rhythmic and repetitive activity that promotes relaxation and stress relief. The release of endorphins during drumming sessions can elevate mood, reduce anxiety, and enhance overall emotional well-being. The rhythmic patterns and vibrations produced by drumming have a soothing effect on the nervous system, leading to a sense of calm and balance.

Lastly, lifelong learning of rhythm and drumming has been linked to improved executive functions. Executive functions encompass a range of cognitive processes, including problem-solving, decision-making, planning, and self-control. Regular drumming practice can enhance these executive functions by requiring individuals to follow complex rhythmic patterns, switch between different drumming techniques, and make real-time decisions based on musical cues. These cognitive demands strengthen executive functions and contribute to improved cognitive flexibility, self-regulation, and overall cognitive performance.

Lifelong learning of rhythm and drumming offers numerous cognitive benefits that extend beyond the realm of music. The cognitive demands of drumming enhance memory, attention, motor skills, language and communication abilities, creativity, problem-solving skills, stress reduction, emotional well-being, and executive functions. Whether you are a beginner or an experienced drummer, the cognitive benefits of rhythm and drumming make it an enriching and fulfilling lifelong pursuit that promotes brain development, cognitive health, and overall well-being.

Emotional Well-being

Drumming has a profound impact on our emotional well-being. It serves as a cathartic outlet for stress and anxiety, allowing us to release tension and experience a sense of release. The rhythmic nature of drumming induces a state of flow, where worries fade away, and we become fully immersed in the present moment.

Embarking on a lifelong journey of learning rhythm and drumming can have profound emotional well-being benefits. The act of drumming itself is a cathartic and expressive experience that allows individuals to tap into their emotions, release pent-up feelings, and find a sense of inner peace. Whether it is playing alone or in a group setting, drumming has a transformative effect on emotional well-being.

One of the key emotional benefits of drumming is stress reduction. Drumming provides a rhythmic and repetitive activity that promotes relaxation and serves as an outlet for emotional tension. The act of striking the drums and creating percussive sounds can be incredibly cathartic, allowing individuals to channel their stress and frustrations into the instrument. Drumming also has a meditative quality that enables individuals to enter a state of flow, where they become fully absorbed in the rhythm and detached from everyday worries and anxieties.

Furthermore, drumming has the power to elevate mood and boost emotional well-being. The release of endorphins during drumming sessions can induce a sense of joy, pleasure, and positivity. The rhythmic patterns and vibrations produced by drumming have a direct impact on the nervous system, promoting relaxation and activating the body's natural feel-good response. Engaging in regular drumming practice can help individuals combat feelings of depression, anxiety, and emotional stagnation, leading to a more balanced and uplifted emotional state.

In addition to stress reduction and mood enhancement, drumming fosters emotional expression and self-awareness. The rhythmic beats of the drums can serve as a non-verbal language through which individuals can express and communicate their emotions. Drumming allows for a release of pent-up feelings, providing a healthy and constructive outlet for emotional expression. By engaging in the act of drumming, individuals can gain a deeper understanding of their emotions, cultivate self-awareness, and develop emotional intelligence.

Drumming also promotes a sense of connection and community,

which contributes to emotional well-being. Participating in drum circles or group drumming sessions creates a shared experience of rhythm and music. The synchronized beats and collective energy generate a sense of unity and belonging. Drumming together with others fosters social connections and a feeling of being part of something greater than oneself. This sense of community can be particularly beneficial for individuals who may feel isolated or disconnected, providing a supportive and inclusive space for emotional expression and connection.

Lifelong learning of rhythm and drumming can enhance resilience and emotional coping skills. Learning and mastering new rhythms, techniques, and musical styles requires perseverance, discipline, and the ability to adapt to challenges. The process of overcoming obstacles and pushing through plateaus fosters resilience and a sense of achievement. Drumming provides a healthy coping mechanism and a creative outlet to navigate and process emotions during difficult times, contributing to emotional strength and well-being.

Embarking on a lifelong journey of learning rhythm and drumming offers numerous emotional well-being benefits. It serves as a powerful stress-reduction tool, elevates mood, fosters emotional expression and self-awareness, promotes a sense of connection and community, and enhances resilience and emotional coping skills. By engaging in the transformative and expressive act of drumming, individuals can cultivate emotional well-being, find solace in rhythm, and experience a deep sense of fulfillment throughout their lifelong journey of musical exploration.

Social Connection

Drumming is often a communal experience, bringing people together in a collective rhythm. Participating in drum circles or joining a band fosters a sense of belonging and camaraderie. It teaches us the value of collaboration, active listening, and synchronizing with others—a reflection of the harmony required in human relationships.

Embarking on a lifelong journey of learning drumming not only offers personal growth but also brings about remarkable social connection benefits. Drumming provides a unique opportunity for individuals to connect with others who share a passion for rhythm and music. As drummers progress in their journey, they have the chance to engage with fellow musicians, join bands, or participate in drum circles, creating a sense of community and forging lasting relationships.

Keith Moon

One of the primary social connection benefits of a lifelong journey of learning drumming is the opportunity for collaboration. Drumming is often a group activity, and participating in ensemble performances or jam sessions requires working together with other musicians. Through collaboration, drummers learn to listen, respond, and synchronize their rhythms with others. This cooperative aspect of drumming fosters teamwork, empathy, and a shared sense of accomplishment. Collaborative drumming experiences strengthen social bonds, create a supportive network, and provide opportunities for mutual growth and learning.

A lifelong journey of learning drumming allows individuals to actively participate in social settings and cultural events. Drummers often become an integral part of musical ensembles, bands, or orchestras, performing in concerts, festivals, or community gatherings. By actively engaging in these social contexts, drummers not only contribute to the collective musical experience but also become part of a broader social network. They connect with fellow musicians, audiences, and enthusiasts, sharing their love for rhythm and drumming, and building relationships that extend beyond the realm of music.

Furthermore, drumming creates a sense of belonging and inclusivity. Drum circles, for example, provide a space where individuals from diverse backgrounds can come together to drum and connect through rhythm. These inclusive settings welcome drummers of all skill levels and cultural backgrounds, fostering a sense of community and breaking down social barriers. Through drumming, people find a shared language that transcends differences, promoting understanding, empathy, and cultural appreciation.

A lifelong journey of learning drumming not only offers personal growth and fulfillment but also brings about significant social connection benefits. Drumming allows individuals to collaborate with fellow musicians, actively participate in social settings, and become part of a broader community. Through drumming, individuals forge lasting relationships, strengthen social bonds, and contribute to a sense of belonging and inclusivity. Whether in ensembles, bands, or drum circles, the social connections formed through a lifelong journey of learning drumming enrich lives and create a supportive network that extends beyond the music itself.

The Beginner's Mindset

Embarking on a musical journey through drumming requires adopting a beginner's mindset—an attitude of openness, curiosity, and humility. Embracing the process of learning, rather than fixating on outcomes, allows us to explore new rhythms, techniques, and musical styles with joy and enthusiasm.

Embarking on a lifelong journey in drumming and music requires cultivating a healthy beginner's mindset. A beginner's mindset is characterized by openness, curiosity, and a willingness to learn and grow. It is an essential mindset to adopt, as it lays the foundation for continuous improvement, creativity, and enjoyment throughout the journey. Here are some key elements of a healthy beginner's mindset in the realm of drumming and music.

Embracing a sense of curiosity is crucial. As a beginner, approaching drumming and music with a curious mindset allows for exploration and discovery. It involves maintaining a genuine interest in learning new techniques, rhythms, and musical concepts. Being curious opens the door to expanding one's musical vocabulary and developing a broader understanding of various genres and styles. Curiosity also encourages experimentation, pushing boundaries, and embracing the unknown, leading to personal growth and artistic development.

A healthy beginner's mindset includes embracing mistakes and failures as opportunities for learning. Learning any instrument, including drums, involves a series of challenges and setbacks. Instead of getting discouraged by mistakes, a beginner's mindset sees them as valuable learning experiences. Each mistake becomes a stepping stone towards improvement and provides valuable feedback for refining technique and musicality. Embracing mistakes with a positive attitude fosters resilience, perseverance, and a continuous drive for self-improvement.

Maintaining patience and celebrating small victories is essential. A lifelong journey in drumming and music is not about immediate mastery but rather about gradual progress and growth. Patience is necessary when faced with technical difficulties or when learning complex rhythms. It involves understanding that progress takes time and that each small achievement should be celebrated. By recognizing and appreciating the incremental improvements, a beginner's mindset remains motivated, energized, and focused on the long-term goals of musical development.

A healthy beginner's mindset is accompanied by a willingness to seek guidance and learn from others. Recognizing that learning is a lifelong process means being open to receiving feedback, taking lessons, and seeking mentorship. Engaging with experienced musicians and drummers fosters a sense of community and provides valuable insights and knowledge. Having a humble attitude and a desire to learn from others' experiences accelerates one's growth and nurtures a sense of camaraderie among fellow musicians.

Adopting a healthy beginner's mindset when embarking on a lifelong journey in drumming and music is extremely crucial for continuous growth and enjoyment. It involves maintaining curiosity, embracing mistakes as learning opportunities, cultivating patience, celebrating small victories, and being open to guidance from others. By embracing this mindset, drummers can unlock their full potential, foster a lifelong love for music, and embark on a fulfilling journey of self-discovery and artistic expression.

Setting Goals

As stated before setting goals is an essential part of lifelong learning. Whether it's mastering a specific drumming technique, learning a complex rhythm, or performing in front of an audience, goals provide direction and motivation. By breaking down larger goals into smaller, achievable milestones, we can track our progress and celebrate incremental victories.

Setting goals can be a valuable tool when embarking on a lifelong journey of learning drumming, rhythm, and music. Goals provide a sense of direction and purpose, guiding musicians through their learning process and keeping them motivated along the way. By setting specific and attainable goals, drummers can structure their practice sessions, measure their progress, and maintain a sense of focus and determination.

Setting goals helps break down the overall journey into smaller, manageable milestones. This approach allows drummers to prioritize their learning objectives and work systematically towards achieving them. Whether it's mastering a particular technique, learning a challenging rhythm, or expanding their musical repertoire, setting goals ensures a sense of progression and provides a roadmap for improvement. By regularly evaluating their progress and adjusting their goals as necessary, drummers can track their growth, stay motivated, and maintain a sense of accomplishment throughout their lifelong journey.

Additionally, goals help drummers stay accountable and maintain a disciplined practice routine. When clear goals are set, it becomes easier to structure practice sessions and allocate time for different aspects of drumming, such as technique, rhythm, musicality, and repertoire. By setting specific practice targets and dedicating regular time to work on them, drummers can develop consistency and discipline in their learning process. This commitment to regular practice reinforces skill development, strengthens focus and concentration, and ensures steady progress in their musical journey.

Setting goals plays a pivotal role when embarking on a lifelong journey of learning drumming, rhythm, and music. Goals provide direction, structure, and motivation, helping drummers break down their overall objectives into smaller, achievable milestones. By setting clear goals, drummers can measure their progress, stay accountable, maintain discipline, and experience a sense of accomplishment as they continue to develop their skills and deepen their understanding of rhythm and music throughout their lifelong journey.

Seeking Mastery

Drumming is an art form that invites a lifelong pursuit of mastery. Embracing continuous improvement and seeking opportunities for growth keeps the journey exciting and fulfilling. Exploring different drumming styles, studying with mentors, attending workshops, and experimenting with improvisation expands our repertoire and deepens our understanding of rhythm.

Embarking on a lifelong journey of learning drumming, rhythm, and music provides an opportunity for musicians to pursue mastery in their craft. Mastery is not just about reaching a destination but rather a continuous pursuit of growth, refinement, and deepening understanding. It involves a commitment to lifelong learning and a passion for constantly pushing the boundaries of one's musical abilities.

One of the key aspects of seeking mastery in drumming and music is a dedication to practice. Mastery requires consistent and deliberate practice, with a focus on refining technique, expanding musical knowledge, and developing a strong sense of rhythm. It involves regular repetition of exercises, challenging oneself with new rhythms and musical styles, and seeking feedback from experienced musicians. By dedicating time and effort to deliberate practice, drummers can progressively refine their skills and move closer to mastery.

Seeking mastery also involves embracing a growth mindset. It is about seeing challenges and setbacks as opportunities for learning and growth. Drummers with a growth mindset approach obstacles with resilience, viewing them as stepping stones towards improvement rather than insurmountable barriers. They actively seek feedback, analyze their performances, and constantly look for ways to enhance their musicality. By maintaining a growth mindset, drummers foster a mindset of continuous improvement and are more likely to reach higher levels of mastery.

Furthermore, seeking mastery in drumming and music requires a deep understanding and appreciation of the art form. Drummers immerse themselves in the study of different musical genres, rhythmic patterns, and drumming techniques. They explore the history and cultural context behind different styles of music, gaining a broader perspective on their instrument and its role in various musical traditions. This deep understanding allows drummers to develop a unique musical voice, incorporating diverse influences and creating their own expressive style.

Seeking mastery in drumming and music involves embracing creativity and pushing the boundaries of musical expression. Drummers who seek mastery are not content with simply reproducing what has been done before but instead strive to create something new and unique. They experiment with different rhythms, explore improvisation, and collaborate with other musicians to push the boundaries of their own musicality. Mastery is not just about technical proficiency but also about finding one's own artistic voice and making a personal statement through music.

Through the lifelong journey of learning drumming, rhythm, and music is a transformative and fulfilling pursuit. It requires dedication to practice, a growth mindset, a deep understanding of the art form, and a commitment to creativity and expression. By embracing these elements, drummers can embark on a lifelong journey of continual growth, pushing the boundaries of their musical abilities, and reaching higher levels of mastery. Ultimately, seeking mastery is not just about becoming a skilled drummer but about fostering a lifelong passion for music and using the drum as a vehicle for personal expression and artistic exploration.

Lifelong learning and the world of drumming intersect in a harmonious symphony of personal growth and self-expression. Through the universal language of rhythm, we connect with ourselves and others on a profound level. The transformative power of drumming in fostering cognitive benefits, emotional well-being, and social connection is a testament to its value as a lifelong learning tool. So, pick up your drumsticks, embrace the rhythm, and embark on a musical journey that will enrich your life indefinitely.

Chapter 10

Motivation vs. Determination: Fueling the Lifelong Journey of Learning Drumming, Rhythm, and Music

Embarking on a lifelong journey of learning drumming, rhythm, and music requires a delicate balance between motivation and determination. While motivation provides the initial spark and enthusiasm, determination serves as the driving force that propels musicians forward, even when faced with challenges and obstacles. In this chapter, we delve into the interplay between motivation and determination, exploring how these two qualities complement each other and contribute to the success and fulfillment of drummers on their lifelong journey of musical growth.

The Spark That Ignites the Flame

Motivation plays a pivotal role at the beginning of the journey, igniting the flame of passion for drumming and music. It is the intrinsic or extrinsic factors that inspire drummers to pick up their sticks, explore new rhythms, and push themselves beyond their comfort zones. Motivation can stem from a deep love for music, the desire for self-expression, the pursuit of mastery, or the admiration of musical idols. It is the fuel that propels drummers to practice, attend lessons, and seek out new musical experiences. While motivation is essential in getting started, it can fluctuate over time, making it necessary to develop a foundation of determination to sustain progress.

Motivation is the driving force that propels individuals to pursue their passions and achieve their goals. When it comes to learning an instrument like the drums and exploring the world of rhythm and music, motivation plays a crucial role in kindling the initial spark that eventually ignites into a burning flame of dedication. In this essay, we will explore the various factors that contribute to the motivation behind learning drums, the significance of rhythm, and how this passion for music ultimately leads to a deeper appreciation for the art form.

Learning the drums offers a unique avenue for personal expression and creativity. The instrument allows individuals to communicate their emotions, thoughts, and experiences through the beats and rhythms they create. The desire to express oneself and channel emotions through music serves as a powerful motivation for aspiring drummers. The sense of accomplishment and self-discovery that comes with developing rhythmic skills fosters a deepening connection to the instrument, amplifying the motivation to learn and grow.

Rhythm is the heartbeat of music, and it forms the foundation of drumming. The inherent human inclination to move to a beat and tap into the innate sense of rhythm acts as a catalyst for learning drums. The experience of syncing with the beat, feeling the vibrations, and creating intricate rhythms generates a sense of joy and fulfillment. The rhythmic patterns produced by drummers have the power to evoke strong emotions and resonate with listeners, making the pursuit of drumming an inherently rewarding and motivating endeavor.

Music has the remarkable ability to bring people together. Learning drums often involves playing alongside other musicians, be it in a band, orchestra, or jamming sessions with fellow enthusiasts. The desire to collaborate, synchronize with others, and create harmonious melodies fuels the motivation to master the instrument. The joy of connecting with like-minded individuals, sharing musical experiences, and contributing to a collective effort strengthens the motivation to learn drums and become an integral part of the musical community.

Drumming, like any other musical instrument, requires discipline, practice, and patience. The process of learning and gradually mastering the complexities of drumming instills a sense of accomplishment and boosts self-confidence. As drummers progress in their journey, the milestones achieved along the way act as motivation to continue pushing boundaries, learning new techniques, and expanding their repertoire. The pursuit of mastery becomes an ongoing source of motivation, fueling the desire to refine skills and explore new horizons in music.

Learning drums provides numerous emotional and cognitive benefits. Playing an instrument is known to reduce stress, improve focus and concentration, and enhance cognitive abilities. The act of drumming releases endorphins, promoting a sense of well-being and providing an outlet for emotional expression. The positive impact on mental health and overall well-being acts as a strong motivation for individuals to engage in the learning process and immerse themselves in the world of music.

Teaching from the road.

Motivation serves as the spark that ignites the flame to learn drums, rhythm, and ultimately music. Personal expression, the joy of rhythm, collaboration, skill development, and the emotional and cognitive benefits associated with drumming all contribute to the motivation behind this artistic pursuit. The passion for music drives aspiring drummers to invest time and effort, leading to a deeper understanding and appreciation of the art form. As the flames of motivation grow brighter, the drummers embark on a lifelong journey of self-discovery, creativity, and musical fulfillment.

Determination: The Steadfast Resolve to Overcome Challenges

Determination is the unwavering resolve to persevere in the face of obstacles and setbacks. Unlike motivation, which can waver, determination remains steadfast, providing the resilience needed to navigate the ups and downs of the lifelong journey. It is the mindset that refuses to give up, even when faced with technical difficulties, creative blocks, or periods of frustration. Determination is developed through discipline, setting goals, and embracing a growth mindset. It is the commitment to consistent practice, the pursuit of improvement, and the belief in one's ability to overcome challenges. With determination as the driving force, drummers can push through plateaus, learn from mistakes, and continue to progress, even when motivation may temporarily wane.

Determination is a powerful force that propels individuals to surmount obstacles and achieve success. When it comes to the realms of drumming, music, and rhythm, determination serves as a driving factor behind the relentless pursuit of mastery. In this essay, we will explore the significance of determination in overcoming challenges, the transformative power it holds for musicians, and how it cultivates resilience and growth in the world of drumming.

Learning to play the drums is a journey that demands persistence and an unwavering commitment to improvement. Challenges abound, from mastering intricate rhythms and coordinating limb movements to developing a keen sense of timing. Determined individuals approach these challenges with an open mind and embrace the learning curve. They recognize that setbacks and obstacles are natural parts of the process, and instead of being discouraged, they use them as stepping stones toward progress. With determination, drummers persistently practice, seeking guidance and refining their skills, refusing to be deterred by initial difficulties.

Drumming is a complex art form that requires coordination, dexterity, and a deep understanding of rhythm. As musicians progress, they encounter increasingly intricate patterns, polyrhythms, and improvisational techniques. Determination is vital in facing these complexities head-on. Drummers with unwavering resolve remain steadfast in their pursuit, patiently breaking down challenging concepts into manageable pieces and gradually integrating them into their repertoire. Their determination fuels a desire to understand and conquer the intricate aspects of drumming, leading to profound growth and mastery.

Failure is an inevitable part of any artistic journey, and drumming is no exception. Mistakes, missed beats, and imperfect performances are opportunities for growth rather than reasons to give up. Determined drummers exhibit resilience in the face of failure, using setbacks as motivation to improve. They acknowledge their weaknesses, seek constructive feedback, and view each setback as a chance to learn and refine their craft. With each setback overcome, their determination solidifies, propelling them forward on their path to success.

Performance anxiety can be a significant challenge for drummers and musicians. The pressure of playing in front of an audience, the fear of making mistakes, and the anticipation of judgment can be overwhelming. Determination empowers musicians to confront and overcome these anxieties. Through consistent practice, mental preparation, and exposure to performance opportunities, drummers develop the resilience necessary to perform under pressure. Their unwavering resolve fuels the courage to step onto the stage, deliver their best, and push past their comfort zones.

Determination in drumming extends beyond the initial stages of learning. It drives drummers to continually seek growth and push the boundaries of their skills. With each milestone achieved, determined musicians set new goals and challenges for themselves. The pursuit of excellence becomes an intrinsic part of their identity. They willingly invest time, effort, and energy into honing their craft, forever striving to reach new levels of musicality. This unwavering commitment to growth and improvement is a testament to their determination and fuels their continued success.

Determination serves as the unwavering resolve that propels drummers and musicians to overcome challenges in the pursuit of excellence. Embracing the learning curve, navigating complexity, cultivating resilience, and confronting performance anxiety are all significant hurdles that determination helps conquer. The journey of drumming is a testament to the transformative power of determination, as it instills resilience, fosters growth, and propels musicians toward ever-greater heights. With determination as their driving force, drummers become living examples of the incredible strength and unwavering resolve it takes to overcome challenges and achieve musical greatness.

The Symbiotic Relationship: Balancing Motivation and Determination

The interplay between motivation and determination is crucial for sustaining long-term growth and fulfillment in drumming and music. While motivation provides the initial drive and excitement, it is determination that carries musicians through the more challenging and demanding phases of the journey. Conversely, determination can be nurtured and reinforced by rekindling motivation through exposure to new musical styles, attending concerts, collaborating with other musicians, or setting new goals. The balance between motivation and determination allows drummers to find joy and purpose in their lifelong pursuit of musical excellence.

When embarking on the journey of learning how to play drums, rhythm, and music, two powerful forces, motivation and determination, work hand in hand to fuel progress and success. Motivation serves as the initial spark that ignites the desire to learn and explore the world of music, while determination provides the unwavering resolve needed to overcome challenges and persevere. In this essay, we will delve into the symbiotic relationship between motivation and determination, highlighting their interdependence and the impact they have on one's musical journey.

Motivation is the driving force that propels individuals to embark on their musical journey. It stems from an inherent passion for music, the desire for self-expression, or an appreciation for the art form. Motivation acts as the catalyst that ignites the initial interest in playing the drums and creating rhythms. It provides the excitement and inspiration needed to take the first step, whether it be enrolling in lessons, acquiring an instrument, or dedicating time to practice. Motivation fuels the initial enthusiasm, creating a sense of purpose and direction.

While motivation initiates the journey, determination sustains and propels progress. Determination is the unwavering resolve to persevere in the face of challenges, setbacks, and obstacles. It is the commitment to overcome difficulties and achieve mastery. When combined with motivation, determination allows aspiring drummers to maintain focus, push through frustration, and stay dedicated to their craft. It provides the resilience needed to navigate the inevitable hurdles encountered along the way and turn them into opportunities for growth.

The relationship between motivation and determination is dynamic, with each influencing and reinforcing the other. Motivation serves as the fuel that energizes determination, while determination helps sustain and enhance motivation. As drummers encounter challenges and obstacles, determination steps in to keep them moving forward. It allows drummers to stay committed, even when motivation wanes. Conversely, when determination feels tested, motivation acts as a reminder of the passion and joy that drew drummers to music in the first place. It helps reignite the fire and enthusiasm needed to push through difficult times.

The symbiotic relationship between motivation and determination paves the way for growth and progress. Motivation provides the initial spark and enthusiasm for learning, while determination ensures consistent effort and practice. As drummers witness their own progress and witness the fruits of their labor, motivation is reinforced, fueling the desire to reach higher levels of proficiency. In turn, determination strengthens as drummers become more invested in their musical journey, setting new goals and embracing challenges. This virtuous cycle of motivation and determination nurtures continuous growth and pushes drummers to surpass their own expectations.

The harmonious interplay between motivation and determination cultivates a lifelong passion for music. As drummers experience the joy of creating rhythms and melodies, the fulfillment of self-expression, and the sense of accomplishment that comes with mastery, their motivation deepens. This enduring motivation, combined with determination, leads to a sustained commitment to learning and refining musical skills. Drummers become lifelong learners, continuously seeking new challenges and avenues for musical expression.

Motivation and determination form a symbiotic relationship that drives individuals to learn how to play drums, rhythm, and music. Motivation provides the initial inspiration and excitement, while determination sustains progress and helps overcome obstacles. Balancing these two forces is essential for a fulfilling musical journey. As motivation fuels the desire to learn and explore, determination provides the unwavering resolve needed to overcome challenges and persevere. When motivation and determination work in harmony, drummers find themselves on a transformative path of growth, self-discovery, and a lifelong passion for music.

In the lifelong journey of learning drumming, rhythm, and music, both motivation and determination play integral roles. While motivation provides the initial spark, determination is the driving force that propels musicians forward, even when faced with difficulties. Balancing these two qualities is crucial for sustaining progress and finding fulfillment in the journey. By cultivating a foundation of determination, drummers can overcome challenges, stay committed to practice and improvement, and reignite their motivation when needed. With motivation as the spark and determination as the guiding light, drummers can navigate the lifelong journey with unwavering passion, purpose, and joy.

Chapter 11
Embrace the Beat Within Through Drums and Rhythm

In this journey of exploring the power of drums and rhythm, we have embarked on a profound and transformative adventure. Through the pulsating beats and melodic cadences, we have discovered a universal language that transcends cultural barriers, connects us on a deeper level, and allows us to express the very essence of our being. In this concluding chapter, we will reflect on the profound impact that drums and rhythm have had on our lives, our communities, and the world at large.

The drum, a primal instrument that has been part of human history since time immemorial, holds a unique place in the heart of humanity. It speaks to us in ways that words cannot, awakening a primal instinct within us, and inviting us to dance, to move, and to connect with the rhythm of life itself. The steady beat of a drum has the power to synchronize our hearts, minds, and bodies, creating a sense of unity and harmony. It has the ability to transport us to a state of pure presence, where worries fade away, and we become one with the music.

Through the act of playing the drums, we have tapped into a wellspring of creativity and self-expression. The rhythmic patterns and drumming techniques we have explored have allowed us to communicate our

emotions, thoughts, and dreams without the need for words. We have discovered the joy of improvisation, the thrill of collaboration, and the transformative power of finding our own unique voice within the rhythm.

Drums and rhythm have proven to be powerful tools for healing and personal growth. We have witnessed firsthand the therapeutic effects of drumming, as it releases stress, promotes relaxation, and helps us connect with our inner selves. In drum circles and communal gatherings, we have experienced the profound sense of belonging and interconnectedness that comes from drumming together, as our individual beats merge into a collective pulse, creating a tapestry of sound that transcends individuality.

Beyond the personal realm, drums and rhythm have played a significant role in cultural preservation and celebration. They have been the heartbeat of communities, carrying the stories, traditions, and histories of diverse cultures across generations. From ancient tribal rituals to modern-day performances, drums have been at the center of ceremonies, festivities, and social gatherings, providing a space for cultural expression, celebration, and unity.

As we look at the world around us, we see the transformative potential of drums and rhythm on a larger scale. They have been utilized as a vehicle for social change and activism, amplifying voices, and inspiring movements. The powerful beats have acted as catalysts for revolutions, advocating for justice, equality, and freedom. They have been instruments of protest and solidarity, uniting people across boundaries, and igniting a collective spirit of resilience and determination.

The journey of embracing the beat within through drums and rhythm has been a testament to the power of music to uplift, connect, and transform. The rhythmic cadences have allowed us to tap into our innate creativity, find solace in the midst of chaos, and forge connections with others on a profound level. They have reminded us that, at our core, we are all part of a universal rhythm, interconnected and interdependent.

So, let us continue to embrace the beat within, not only through drums and rhythm but through the rhythm of life itself. Let us dance to the melodies that surround us, finding harmony within ourselves and with others. Let us celebrate our diversity, knowing that our unique beats contribute to the symphony of humanity. And let us remember, always, that in the midst of the chaos and cacophony of the world, the beat of our hearts and the rhythm of our souls guide us toward our truest selves.

About the Author

Bart Robley is a multi-talented drummer, author, educator, and recording artist who has made significant contributions to the world of music. Born and raised on a cattle ranch in the picturesque Deer Creek canyon area of Littleton, Colorado, Bart developed a deep love for rhythm and music from a young age. With his relentless pursuit of excellence and dedication to his craft, Bart has established himself as a prominent figure in the drumming community.

Bart's passion for drums led him to seek guidance from some of the industry's finest mentors. Over the years, he has studied under renowned drummers such as Gregg Bissonette, Ralph Humprey, Dave Lombardo, Rob Hesskett, Dom Famularo, and Robert Slack. These experiences allowed Bart to refine his skills and expand his musical horizons, honing his technique and deepening his understanding of rhythm.

For over two decades, Bart has been an integral part of The Sam Morrison Band, a testament to his exceptional talent and dedication. With his dynamic drumming style, Bart has contributed to the band's success, enhancing their performances and captivating audiences with

his skillful and energetic playing.

In addition to his contributions as a performing artist, Bart is also an accomplished author and educator. His expertise in drumming has allowed him to share his knowledge with aspiring drummers through his instructional materials and workshops. Bart's ability to break down complex concepts and communicate them in a clear and accessible manner has earned him recognition as a sought-after educator.

Bart's talent and contributions to the music industry have not gone unnoticed. In 2009, his exceptional skills were recognized with a Telly Award, a prestigious honor bestowed upon individuals who demonstrate outstanding creativity and excellence in the field of media production.

Throughout his career, Bart Robley has remained committed to his art, consistently pushing the boundaries of his abilities and inspiring others with his passion for drums, rhythm, and music. His journey from the tranquil ranches of Colorado to becoming a revered drummer, author, educator, and recording artist is a testament to his unwavering dedication and the profound impact he has made in the world of music.

Bart Robley Proudly Endorses

Gretsch®

Sabian

Gibraltar

Vic Firth®

Aquarian® Drumheads

Trick Drums ★ USA

Kickport®

The Kelly SHU Pro™

Humes & Berg Mfg. Co., Inc.

Audix Microphones

Friends from the Back Cover

Gregg Bissonette is an American jazz and rock drummer and vocalist. He is the brother of bassist Matt Bissonette, with whom he frequently collaborates. He has played on albums by dozens of recording artists, including David Lee Roth's first three solo albums. He has been a member of Ringo Starr and his All Starr Band since 2008.

As the current drummer for Dwight Yoakam, **Mitch Marine** calls Los Angeles his home, where he plays, writes and produces music. He is an established country rock drummer, bridging the gap between the two styles of music with his upbeat rhythm and stylish flair.

Chris Brady is the Artist Relations Director for Aquarian Drumheads in Anaheim, CA. Aquarian was founded in the 1980s by the legendary Roy Burns.

More Great Books from Bart Robley...

DRUMMER'S SURVIVAL GUIDE
00001331 Book $12.99

SCHOOL OF HARD ROCKS
00001214 DVD $24.95

ROCKIN' POPPIN' SNARE DRUM
00001562 Book $19.99

ASAP DRUM SETUP
00001293 DVD $10.99

SCHOOL OF HARD ROCKS
00001203 Book $15.95

ASAP RUDIMENTAL DRUMMING
00001332 DVD $19.99

CENTERSTREAM®

P.O. Box 17878 - Anaheim Hills, CA 92817
(714) 779-9390 www.centerstream-usa.com